# ON STAGE

First published 1993 by
Merlion Publishing Ltd
2 Bellinger Close
Greenways Business Park
Chippenham
Wiltshire SN15 1BN
UK

Consultant: Günter Berghaus PhD
Editors: Caroline Bingham, Karen Foster, Josephine Paker
Designers: Jane Brett, Tracy Carrington, Paul Fielder
Cover designer: Tracy Carrington
Picture researcher: Claire Allen
Typesetting co-ordinator: Gina Brierley



Printed in Great Britain by BPCC Paulton Books Ltd.

ISBN 1 85737 003 1

Artwork on pages 14/15, 30, 107 and 159 by Sarah Lever; pages 23, 27 32/33, 58/59, 71, 103, 108, 122/123, 138/139, 141 and 174 by Kiki Lewis (B L Kearley Ltd) and on pages 8, 25, 40, 42, 67, 69, 77, 81, 96/97, 110, 118, 135, 137 and 175 by Andrew Midgley.

Models on pages 35, 91, 151 and 157 by Jane Brett; page 69 and 99 by Tracy Carrington; page 149 by Paul Fielder; page 113 and 183 by Beverly Knowlden and on pages 13, 22/23, 27, 32/33, 57, 77, 98/99, 105, 127, 129, 131 and 181 by Sarah Lever.

Photographs on pages 106/107, 109, 111 and 154 by Bernard Brandham and on pages 3, 13, 17, 22/23, 26/27, 32/33, 35, 38/39, 47, 48/49, 52/53, 57, 63, 69, 72, 77, 78/79, 80/81, 83, 84/85, 87, 89, 90/91, 92/93, 94/95, 97, 98/99, 102/103, 105, 110, 113, 115, 116/117, 121, 125, 126/127, 128/129, 130/131, 149, 150/151, 152/153, 154/155, 157, 158/159, 162/163, 164/165, 168/169, 172/173, 178/179, 180/181, 182/183, 184/185, 186/187, 188/189 and 190/191 by Mike Stannard.

MERLION ARTS LIBRARY

# ON STAGE

Contributors:
**Michael Pollard**
Caroline Bingham
Josephine Paker

# CONTENTS

CHAPTER FOUR



CHAPTER FIVE



CHAPTER SIX

# CHAPTER ONE

# DRAMA THROUGH THE AGES

People have always celebrated events that are important in their lives. Thousands of years ago these celebrations took place outside and they often included dance and drama. People would gather together to celebrate a successful hunt, or a good harvest. Small groups would perform a celebratory dance. The idea of theatre was born.

In this chapter you'll discover how people's ideas of theatrical performance, or drama, have changed throughout the ages. And you can bring history into your own home by making a harlequin shirt, similar to the shirts worn by the Italian commedia dell'arte performers in the 1500s. Or why not make a Wild Man's wreath, used by English mummers in the 1600s? Very soon you will be putting on your own performances from the past!

# Dramatic beginnings

What is the meaning of life? What causes the sun to shine? Where do we come from? People have been asking questions like these for thousands of years. But long ago there were no scientists around to offer answers. And there were no religious leaders to offer a meaning either. So people overcame their fear of nature and the unknown by creating gods and spirits. They gave personalities to the wind, to the earth, even to each separate tree. The Ancient Greeks, for example, worshipped many gods and goddesses, among them Poseidon, the god of the sea, and Demeter, the goddess of harvests.

In olden days, people used to perform dances and rituals to ask their gods and spirits to bring them good luck. They danced before they went hunting or blessed the land before planting seeds. Even today, some people still feel close to nature in this way. Here you see an African tribe in Zaire performing a dance which goes way back through their history. The dancers wear masks representing the spirits.

In Ancient Egypt, the rituals told stories about the gods and involved chanting prayers and reciting poetry.

Rituals like these probably formed the beginnings of modern theatre. There was, however, one major difference. Since everybody took part in a ritual, there was no one left to watch – there was no audience. True theatre only developed as some people deliberately began to act out stories for groups of spectators. They pretended to be other people, or imitated the actions of gods, or animals, to entertain an audience.

This ancient ritual dance is being performed in Zaire

These men are performing a dance-drama in Bali, Indonesia

## Dance and drama

What's the difference between dancing and acting out a drama? In many countries the two kinds of entertainment are so closely linked it's difficult to separate them. This picture shows a performance of a dance-drama on the Indonesian island of Bali. This is a monkey dance which tells part of the story behind an ancient Hindu poem called the Ramayana.

Over the years, different versions of the Ramayana have developed all over the Eastern world. But they have one thing in common – they involve both dancing and acting. The links between dance and drama run through many other types of theatrical performance, as you will find out as you read this book.

# Ancient Greek theatres

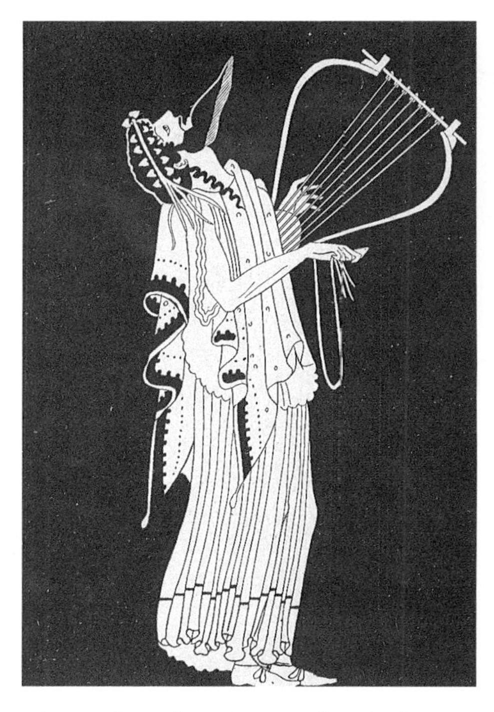

A member of an Ancient Greek chorus

Close your eyes! You've been transported back 2,500 years and you're sitting on the side of a hill outside the great city of Athens in Greece. It is dawn on a misty April morning. Around you, the hillsides slope down to form a bowl shape and, as you watch, groups of people from the city begin to gather. There are a few rows of wooden benches for people to sit on. The crowd waits in hushed excitement.

Below, in the centre of the bowl, there is an empty area of flattened earth. As the light grows, 15 singers dressed in colourful costumes file into the area and take up their positions. These singers are called the chorus. Once they are all gathered, they start to dance, sing and chant. One member of the chorus carries a lyre, a stringed instrument, which he begins to pluck. Then the actors appear. You are about to hear how the Greeks won a great victory in battle.

This vase painting depicts members of an Ancient Greek chorus

The theatre at Epidaurus in Greece

## Stone theatres

In later years, the Greeks built special open-air arenas, or amphitheatres, where they could stage their plays. These were more or less the same shape as the natural hillside bowls, but they contained rows of stone seats for the audience – for perhaps as many as 20,000 people! The seats formed a horseshoe shape, and the rows sloped steeply upwards so that everyone would have a good view of the actors. The flattened central area was replaced by a raised stage. Behind it a building was erected which served as a backdrop for the play and as dressing-rooms for the actors. It was also a sounding-board, helping to project the sound of the actors' voices to every part of the huge arena.

We know what these theatres were like because you can still see the ruins of some of them today. You can sit on the same hard stones that served as seats all those years ago. You'll be amazed how easily you can hear what someone down in the arena is saying. At Epidaurus in southern Greece, the theatre that was built 2,200 years ago has been restored to its original state. You can see it in the picture above. Ancient Greek plays are performed at Epidaurus every summer.

# Choosing the best

This vase painting depicts an Ancient Greek satyr play

The people of Ancient Greece loved theatrical performances, and held drama festivals every year for everyone to enjoy. The festivals were actually competitions intended to find the very best playwrights in the country. The main festival in Athens was called the City Dionysia and it lasted for four days every March or April.

## Entering the competition

Each of the competitors wrote four plays for the competition, usually three tragedies and one satyr play, a kind of comedy. The judges chose the best to be performed in the festival. You can see an artist's impression of a Greek satyr play in the picture above.

## Fame

Prizes were awarded to the writers of the best tragedy and comedy, to the best production, and to the best actor. But for the writers the most important thing was to win at the festival and make their name. Afterwards their plays would be famous and in demand in other cities.

## The Greek performers

On stage all the female parts were taken by men. They wore masks so that the audience could tell immediately which part they were playing. The masks looked something like the two faces pictured here. The only performer who didn't wear a mask was the pipe player who accompanied the chanting chorus. He would have found it difficult to blow an instrument through a mask!

The actors were all professional performers and were paid by the state. The chorus were usually paid by some generous, wealthy citizen. Altogether, the drama festival was a magnificent way of entertaining huge numbers of people, and certainly as popular as a major pop festival today. Thousands of people attended the plays, flocking from all over the city to watch. The state even paid a small allowance to the poorer citizens to enable them to buy a seat.

Two reconstructions of Ancient Greek performance masks

A modern performance of the *Oresteia* by the Ancient Greek playwright Aeschylus

## The winners

The Greek playwright, Aeschylus, was one of the earliest competitors in the City Dionysia. He was a winner thirteen times. Another winner was Sophocles, who gained eighteen prizes. Euripides, who wrote mainly tragedies, was a prizewinner five times. All these playwrights are still admired and appreciated today, over 2,000 years later. A modern production of one of Aeschylus' plays, the *Oresteia*, is pictured on the right.

## Make your own special prize

You might like to get together with a group of friends, and divide into twos and threes to perform a number of short scenes, or sketches. Why not copy the Greek idea and create a special prize for the best performance.

We made our prize from a paper plate, gluing string on to create a raised design and then spraying it with gold paint. A few beads were glued onto the plate later to give it a smarter look. Ask a group of adults to judge the winners.

# The Romans

This mosaic from Pompeii, Italy, shows a group of actors preparing for a Roman satyr play

About 2,000 years ago, the Romans took over from the Greeks as the most powerful nation on the Mediterranean Sea. They borrowed many Greek ideas, among them Greek forms of drama. This mosaic shows a group of Roman actors preparing for a satyr play. Can you see the masks? Like the Greeks, the Romans made use of masks, but they introduced very different characters into their plays. The Greeks liked to hear ideas discussed on stage and although their plays included music and dancing, the words were more important. The Romans preferred action.

At first, Greek comedies were rewritten by Roman playwrights such as Plautus or

Terence, and given Roman characters and Roman settings. But the Roman audiences did not like these plays, finding them too tame and uninteresting, and so they used the theatres to stage more popular kinds of entertainment. One of these was called the pantomimus.

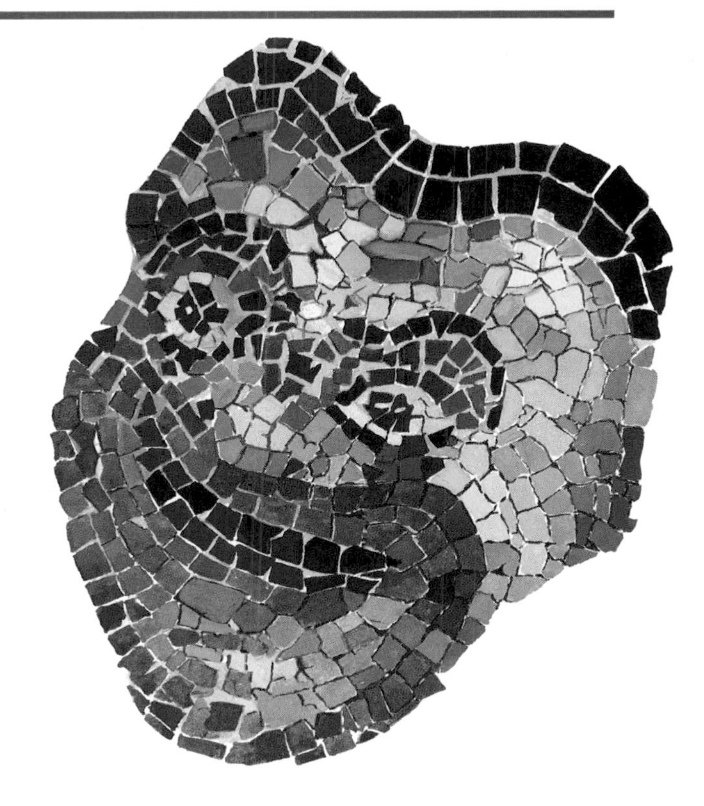

## A silent performer

The pantomimus was a one-man show supported by musicians and a chorus to chant the story. The principal actor mimed the performance, changing his mask each time he played a different character. A comic mask is pictured in this illustration of a Roman mosaic. Look at its closed mouth. The performer didn't speak from behind the mask, nor could you see his facial expressions. He communicated by gestures, by dance and by movement – especially hand movements.

## From farce to spectacle

Farce is a form of comedy which is full of jokes and funny misunderstandings. It also includes slapstick, a boisterous kind of comedy in which people bump into each other and fall over a lot. This vase is decorated with a painting showing a typical Roman farce. The man lying across the chest is pretending to be a miser. He is desperately trying to protect his hoard of treasure from thieves.

The Romans loved farce, but public taste went from bad to worse! The audiences started to demand more outrageous amusement, the ruder and more shocking the better. They didn't want drama any more, they wanted spectacle. They enjoyed chariot racing, and gruesome fights to the death between two gladiators. Acrobats performed daring feats of strength and agility, while criminals battled against lions and tigers. The Romans even flooded the amphitheatres and staged mock sea-battles. No wonder the old-fashioned Greek forms of drama seemed dull!

This vase painting shows an Ancient Roman satyr play

# Indian classics

The Ancient Greeks were not the only people who held competitions to reward the best playwrights. The Indians did as well. But they did not award prizes to the playwrights – they praised the actors instead. Many of these actors were members of the royal courts in India, and the rulers, called the rajahs, did much of the judging themselves.

Sanskrit was the language of India up to some 1,000 years ago. People don't speak it any more, but much of the drama and poetry performed in the Indian theatre was written in Sanskrit. Religious plays in Sanskrit used dance and music to recount the romantic adventures of Hindu gods and princes. There were ten kinds of drama, three different shapes of stage, and many rules about how the plot could be constructed. There were also rules to follow on acting style, facial expression, body movement and language. Each gesture and movement had a particular meaning.

## Heroes and villains

Two early Sanskrit plays are still popular today. One of these is *The Little Clay Cart*, and was probably written by a man called Sudraka. He was a rajah, a mathematician and a skilled elephant

Three scenes from *The Little Clay Cart*

trainer. *The Little Clay Cart* has lots of characters. There's the hero, the heroine, and the villain, as well as a whole cast of gamblers, rogues and clowns. There are ten sections to the play, and the storyline zig-zags through them. Each section is almost long enough to be a complete play. *The Little Clay Cart* is basically a love story. An over-generous merchant falls in love with a rich and beautiful lady. The king's jealous brother-in-law tries to kill the merchant so he can then blame the king for the murder. But his evil plot backfires, and his wickedness is exposed. Indian audiences like happy endings!

## A love story

*Sakuntala*, another Sanskrit play, also has a happy ending. It was written by the most brilliant and best-known of the Sanskrit playwrights, Kalidasa. The story is taken from mythology and tells of a beautiful young girl called Sakuntala who marries a king. Because of a magic curse, the king forgets all about her. Sakuntala is heart-broken. After many adventures, the king regains his memory, and is reunited with Sakuntala. *Sakuntala* has been popular ever since it was written hundreds of years ago. Its traditional acting and beautiful poetry still appeal to modern Indian audiences.

# Church drama

This drawing shows the first woman playwright, a nun called Hrotswitha

Around AD 500, theatre doors in Europe remained firmly closed. Christianity had a strong hold at this time and its leaders considered plays to be shocking, evil and corrupt.

For hundreds of years Christians were not allowed to have anything to do with acting. Entertainers such as acrobats, dancers and singers still went around towns and villages staging their shows, but serious drama didn't exist. However, strangely, it was the Christian church itself that was responsible later on for reviving the theatrical tradition.

## Bringing the Bible to life

Very few people knew how to read around the year AD 900. There were no printed books and news had to be communicated by word of mouth. The only way to get the message of the Bible across was to have the stories acted out by someone. Acting out biblical scenes was a good way of making the stories more lively and interesting, and certain enthusiastic priests began to produce religious plays with actors. The first female playwright we know of lived in the 900s. She was a German nun called Hrotswitha and she decided that short

This painting shows the separate stage settings put up at Valenciennes in 1547

religious plays were an excellent way of interesting people in the Bible. You can see Hrotswitha in the black-and-white picture on the left.

## Performing church dramas

These religious plays proved to be very popular, and in time they grew longer and more complicated. They were performed at church festivals such as Christmas or Easter, and were often staged inside a church building. Many churches had a ready-made stage at one end where the altar stood. However, in the larger churches, there was room to build one or two temporary platforms away from the main stage where distant scenes could take place – such as the shepherds watching in the hills in the Christmas story.

The idea of different platforms grew in popularity and led to different scenes being played on separate stages, or mansions, as they were commonly known.

This painting shows a magnificent series of mansions which were erected at Valenciennes in France in 1547. One mansion represents heaven, where angels dance to the sound of beautiful music. At the other end is hell, complete with devils guarding their unfortunate prisoners. The mansions' system made it easy to put on a play with many different scenes, without having to wait for scenery to be shifted. The audience simply had to turn and face a different area when the actors moved across.

## Moving out of the church

In the larger churches, the main porch and steps could be used as a stage with the audience watching from outside. Out in the open, the actors felt free to introduce more humour. They didn't feel they had to stick so closely to Bible stories. In most European towns and cities, it was only a short step from the church to the market place – and that was where the theatre moved next.

Behind the scenes of a mystery play in the 1500s

# Mystery plays

Imagine you are a member of the audience watching this play. Remember, all you can see is the opening and the costumed actors. But you can hear a tremendous racket! Just look what is going on behind the scenes. Stagehands are banging drums and blowing trumpets, while two small cannons are about to fire. Somebody is banging a huge metal cooking pot. On top of all this, the drummers are shouting as loudly as they can! The scene is one of mayhem, yet everybody appears to know what they are doing. In fact, the stage setting is a representation of hell, and the production is a mystery play.

## Popularizing Christianity

In the 1500 years after the death of Jesus Christ, Christianity spread throughout Europe into every aspect of everyday life. At that time, church services were held in Latin, a language which most people did not understand. The Bible, too, was read out in Latin. The idea grew of teaching stories from the Bible by performing plays in the language the people spoke every day, not in Latin. These were called mystery plays.

## Spectacular messages

One of the earliest and most spectacular mystery plays is the French *Mystère d'Adam*, which was first staged on a church porch around 1170. This play ends with some devils dragging Adam and Eve off to hell. As they do so, smoke belches onto the stage, accompanied by a great clattering of pots and pans! In another French play, the devils put a woman into a cauldron to cook her. After a while, they taste her to see if she's done. She's not, so in disgust they let her go! The devil characters in mystery plays are always punished in the end, and Christ succeeds in rescuing all the people trapped in hell.

These actors are using a cart to recreate a mystery play

## Mansions

While some mystery plays were acted on church steps, others were performed on a series of mansions which were normally positioned around the town square. Sometimes the mansions were mounted on carts which were wheeled around, the actors taking it in turn to perform to different groups of people in the town. These could be very simple, like the cart pictured here, or they could be very elaborate. You can find out more about these carts on pages 90 and 91.

# Travelling entertainers

Look at this lively picture of an entertainer leaping down the road. Can you count how many different things he is carrying? It's not surprising that one of them has smashed on the ground!

Entertainers like this travelled around Europe between the 1200s and 1400s. They carried all their equipment with them, and were ready to perform any one of a number of acts to suit different audiences. One day, they might play to an audience of local people who had come to market. The next, they might perform after a banquet to the family and friends of a rich landowner.

## Minstrels

The travelling entertainers were called minstrels. They dressed in colourful costumes so that people would notice them when they came to town, either on their own or in groups of two or three. A good minstrel learned all sorts of talents. He could sing, dance, recite poetry, play instruments, act and tell stories. Some could do acrobatics, or juggle, or work puppets. Minstrels were nearly always men, since acting was not considered to be a suitable job for a woman.

A travelling entertainer

An African minstrel

## Story-telling

Travelling entertainers performed to audiences all round the world. In many countries, minstrels journeyed from village to village, entertaining people as they went. In Senegal and Mali, in West Africa, they were called griots. Griots still perform today. They sing, tell stories, and dance to the kora, a kind of harp. Other minstrels use tambourines or drums to accompany their tales. You can see an African entertainer at work in the picture above.

## Entertainment in Korea

In Korea, travelling minstrels were known as kwangdaes. They needed a strong, powerful voice. Part of the kwangdae's training was to go to a remote hillside and shout at the top of his voice! The kwangdae's performance was called a p'ansori. All that was needed to put on a p'ansori was a drummer and a mat, so the performance could take place anywhere – often in the open air. Kwangdaes who didn't succeed in the musical side of the entertainment became acrobats or tight-rope walkers. P'ansori is still popular today. You can even see it on television sometimes.

## Make a minstrel's tambourine

It's easy to make a tambourine like those used by the griots. Cut a hole in a tin foil dish and glue a piece of tracing paper into this hole to form a membrane. Then glue two dishes together – you could put small stones inside to give a rattle. Cut discs from the discarded centre of the dish and string these onto the edge of your tambourine. We made a second tambourine from an old chocolate box, cutting holes in the side of the box and threading discs onto matchsticks before gluing the matchsticks behind the holes.

# Nō theatre

In 1375, a 12-year-old Japanese boy called Zeami Motokiyo and his father went to work for the noble warrior Yoshimitsu. But Zeami was not to work as a servant. He was an actor, and he was to become very famous. Once at court, Zeami and his father developed a new kind of drama. They called this drama Nō. Nō is remarkable because it has survived in its original form to this day.

From the first performance, Nō drama was a serious and stylized affair. The stories were all taken from myths and legends as well as from Japanese history and normally told of some tragic event. Nō quickly became popular among the ruling nobles and warrior generals, or samurai, of Japan. In fact, by the 1600s Nō was the only form of Japanese drama which the ruling classes were allowed to go and see. It was considered to be respectable.

A Japanese Kyogen mask

## A Nō performance

Zeami Motokiyo wrote a manual all about Nō plays. The rules he laid down are still followed. Zeami encouraged the performers to make each play seem fresh and new, so although there are 'rules', each performance is always slightly different from any other.

Nō performers are traditionally men, although some of them have to act female parts. There are usually two chief roles. One actor plays the part of a god or hero and always wears a mask. If you see a Nō play, you will find it is acted out at a slow pace. There are not many words, for the plot is told partly in poetry sung by a chorus of ten male voices. The principal performers add speeches, songs and dances of their own.

These actors are performing a Nō drama

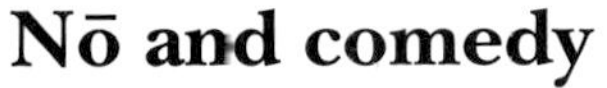

## Nō and comedy

Nō plays are short and so most theatre groups perform three in one evening. As you can imagine it's not much fun watching three tragedies, one after the other, so the three plays are usually broken up by comic sketches called Kyogen. Kyogen are performed by a different set of actors, and they make the evening a lot livelier. A Kyogen mask is pictured on the opposite page.

## A Nō stage

Today, Nō plays are performed in specially constructed buildings, although the stage design has remained the same since the 1600s. This diagram shows a typical Nō stage. Actors enter and exit along the passageway which runs behind three fir trees. A fir tree is also painted on the backcloth. The stage itself is a raised wooden platform with three steps leading up to it, though these are never used. The performers always take the same positions – a group of musicians sits at the back, while the chorus sits to the right. What role do you think the man seated near the passageway takes? Believe it or not, he's just a stagehand, and he is always visible to the audience.

# Mummers

This picture shows a troupe of mummers providing Christmas entertainment in the 1500s

Watch out! The Wild Man is coming. Have you ever heard stories of the Wild Man? By tradition, he was a wood spirit who lived in a deep and very dark forest. He had long, unruly hair and his green clothing looked as if it was made from leaves. He was powerful and carried an uprooted tree as a club. He wasn't a character you would want to meet and certainly not one to be trifled with!

## The Wild Man comes to town

If you had lived in Europe in the 1400s and 1500s, the Wild Man would have been a familiar figure. He would appear in the streets at special festivals in the form of an actor in costume. He danced along with a group of masked companions, collecting money and sweet treats. This merry band even danced into people's homes, where, because they expected payment, they were not always very welcome!

The Wild Man was funny but a bit frightening too. He played an important part in the winter festivities that were held each year to bring rich harvests and good luck to the people. The members of the masked band who accompanied the Wild Man were known as mummers.

## A mumming play

Mummers always performed a mumming play. The play's story, or plot, was very simple. The brave Christian hero, Saint George, had to battle with a wicked knight. One of them was killed, but a doctor would then appear to bring the dead man back to life. Sometimes Saint George had to kill a dragon as well.

You can see a group of mummers in action in the large hall pictured on the left. Can you spot the Wild Man?

The dragon is easy to find, though it doesn't look particularly fierce. It seems more interested in chasing the monkey than in fighting Saint George! You can see Saint George towards the back of the hall, sitting on a white horse.

## Make a Wild Man's wreath

Why not make a Wild Man's wreath to wear on your head! Measure a piece of elastic to fit around your head, then ask an adult to help you sew it into a band. Next, cut leaf shapes from card and paper. You could even cut up a green plastic bag. Attach all these to the head band with sticky tape. You will need to add a lot of leaves – your head should look like an overgrown bush!

# Chinese open-air theatres

Down by the river which runs through a busy town in China, people are beginning to gather to chat and drink tea. There is a great air of excitement. The theatre has come to town.

China is a huge country. Millions of its people live in farming villages many hundreds of miles from any large town or city. Throughout the spring and summer, the farm crops have to be tended and harvested and certainly there's no time to watch plays. But when the season is over, groups of actors take their shows to the villages. Many of the actors may have spent the farming season working in the local fields. Acting is their way of making a living during the autumn and winter.

## Temporary stages

For hundreds of years, these travelling actors have performed on makeshift open-air stages like those on the opposite page. The top illustration was drawn in the 1700s. This stage is made from planks of wood which are resting on a frame of bamboo poles. A carved wooden balcony and shaped roof help make it look smarter.

Stages like this were set up in any number of places. Sometimes a rich landowner or merchant would pay for the performance, and a stage would be set up in front of his house. Otherwise, the actors would build their stage in the village market place. The travelling groups were larger than those that

toured Europe, because they included a team of people whose job it was to build and take down the elaborate stage.

## Old and new

Compare the illustration of the early Chinese stage with the photograph of a modern temporary stage. There's not really a lot of difference. Both stages rest on stilts and contain a screened-off area to provide space for dressing and making up. The audience still stand in groups, though the modern theatre troupe has provided boxes and planks for people to sit on if they wish. There is one important difference! Can you spot the tea-seller in the top picture? Tea-sellers often used to circulate during the performance of a Chinese play. As the plays could last from midday until sunset, refreshments must have been very welcome.

This detail from a scroll painting shows a Chinese open-air theatre in the 1700s

A modern Chinese open-air theatre

# On the road

You have read about entertainers who travel from place to place to find an audience, but can you imagine the problems of carrying everything around with you? Travelling entertainers have to be able to store their everyday clothes along with all the things they might need on stage, from make-up and costumes to small pieces of furniture. They need to travel light, packing everything into a small space, so they take along as little as possible and make use of anything and everything they find along the way.

Take a look at this picture by the Dutch painter Pieter Brueghel the Younger. It shows a European village festival taking place in the street some 400 years ago. A group of travelling actors have set up a temporary stage in a market place, using planks placed on barrels and cloth screens. They are presenting their play to an appreciative audience. They have a table and chair, and are borrowing a stool from a member of the town.

## A loaded wagon

Had you travelled the roads of Europe at this time, you might well have met up with a party of five or six poorly-dressed men with a horse and wagon. The wagon would have been laden with planks of wood, screens, and a few sacks and wooden boxes. They would have been travelling actors taking their plays to the small towns of Europe.

This painting is by the Flemish artist Pieter Brueghel the Younger

They might have asked you what you knew of the towns along the road. In some places, the priest did not allow actors to perform. In other towns, the people disliked strangers and drove them away with stones. Travelling players lived uncertain and sometimes dangerous lives.

But in a friendly town such as the one in Brueghel's picture, the actors would find a space where a crowd could gather – often the market square – and unpack their wagon. The wagon held all they needed, and could even provide the actors with a changing area. Sometimes, an actor standing high up on a ladder behind the curtain would make an unexpected appearance by popping his head over the top.

The plays these actors performed were versions of old, well-known stories. The audience liked stories about goodies and baddies, with plenty of fighting between the two – the more fights, the better! If the audience was happy the actors' pockets would be filled. Or they might be given a few chickens or a fat capon to see them on their way to another town.

# Orta-oyunu

A performance of orta-oyunu

Orta-oyunu is a form of comic theatre that was once very popular in Turkey and the Middle East. Orta-oyunu means middle show, and is so called because the shows were performed in the middle of courtyards and squares. The actors just roped off an area, placed a chair near one end, and a screen at the other end, and began their show.

## A comic tradition

Orta-oyunu is linked both to comic plays found in India, and to the commedia dell'arte which developed in Italy in the 1500s. The plays included music, dancing and acrobatics. The story, or plot, was not very important in orta-oyunu. It was the crazy conversation between the two principal characters that got the audience laughing.

The main character was called Pişekar. He opened the play, and stayed on stage nearly all the time. But when he had nothing to do, he sometimes sat among

the audience. He wore bright red trousers, a yellow gown and a multi-coloured night-cap. He carried a short stick called a cudgel which he used to hit the other main character, Kavuklu. This always made the audience roar with laughter. The characters made fun of people who lived in other parts of Turkey, and mimicked the way they spoke. They were sometimes so rude that they were fined or put in prison!

## The simplest props

The objects needed for an open-air performance of orta-oyunu were very simple – just a chair and a screen. The screen represented the scenery. Pictures were stuck onto the screen to show where the action was taking place. A picture of hills would show that the actors were in the mountains, or windows might indicate the actors were at home.

You could adapt this idea for a performance of your own. Instead of having to find the props and objects you need, you could glue pictures onto cards, which could be held up so that the audience could see. All you need are pictures cut out of magazines, or pictures you have painted yourself, scissors, card and glue. What could be easier!

# The Italian comedians

A scene from a commedia dell'arte performance

Anyone living in Italy in the 1500s and 1600s, would immediately recognize the scene pictured above as commedia dell'arte. This form of comedy was widely liked at this time. The actors wore colourful costumes, and their shows consisted of plenty of corny jokes and knockabout humour, and lots of improvisation. Everybody enjoyed going to see commedia dell'arte.

## A portable stage

Commedia dell'arte actors were trained professionals who organized themselves into travelling groups, carrying their stage and equipment with them. At first the stage was a simple platform, probably a little like the one shown in Brueghel's painting on page 31. The actors performed in front of a painted backcloth which might show a forest scene, a stormy sea, or a city street. It might even show nothing at all, like the one shown in the picture on the left. These backcloths could be rolled up or down so that the scene could change as the play went along.

As time went on, commedia dell'arte productions became more elaborate. Flat pieces of scenery called wings, from which the actors entered and exited, were added at the sides of the stage. And the stages were built on a larger and larger scale. By the 1700s, most commedia dell'arte took place in permanent venues.

## Spread of popularity

Although commedia dell'arte began in northern Italy, it soon spread to other countries in Europe. Royal households, bored with the dull and wordy plays put on for their entertainment, demanded to see commedia dell'arte shows instead. They were performed at the Imperial Court in Vienna, in Spain, France, and even as far away as Russia. They were special favourites of King Louis XIV of France. On their way to these grand venues, the actors would pay for the journey by performing in the towns they passed through along the way.

One of the things the people liked about commedia dell'arte was that the characters were always the same, and they were instantly recognisable. You can recognize Arlecchino in the picture by his multi-coloured costume – this was usually patterned with diamonds. Arlecchino is also known as Harlequin, and you will find a picture of him if you turn to page 101. You can read more about the other characters in commedia dell'arte on the next pages.

## Make your own Harlequin costume

Many of the performers who played Harlequin made their own costumes by stitching diamond-shaped pieces of fabric onto their clothes. If you're invited to a fancy-dress party and want to act the clown, you would certainly look the part in this Harlequin shirt. Cut the diamond shapes from brightly-coloured material, and use a different coloured thread to stitch them onto the shirt. Add a mask for extra effect. You could even make a hat from strong paper and feathers.

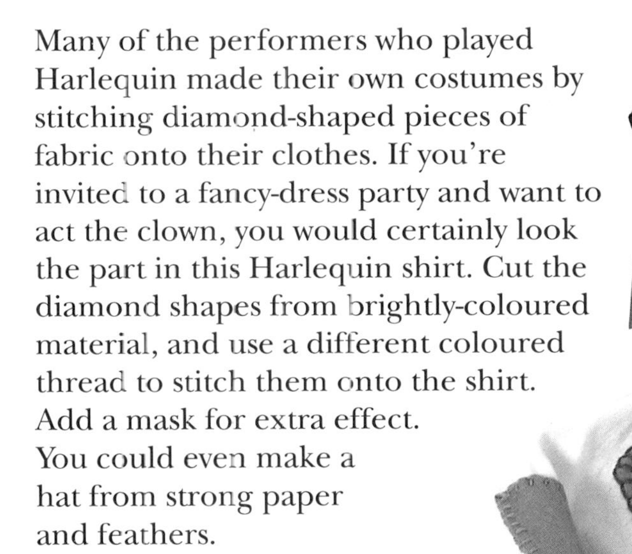

# Some zany characters

It was 1570, and Catherine de Medici, a princess of the ruling family of Florence and mother of the King of France, was feeling homesick. She longed for a reminder of her beloved home in Italy which she had left 37 years before. So she sent for a troupe of Italian commedia dell'arte actors in the sure knowledge that they would be able to cheer her up. After all, commedia dell'arte was all about laughing.

## Set scenes

Commedia entertainment always consisted of a series of set situations. A list of these, called the scenario, was pinned up in the actors' dressing area, so they knew exactly what was going to happen. There were two zanni, or clowns, who were usually servants. This is where the modern word 'zany' comes from. One of these clowns was a crafty rascal called Brighella, the other was a dim-witted fool called Arlecchino or Harlequin. Brighella is pictured here. There were always two pompous, middle-aged men, usually a merchant called Pantaleone and a doctor. Other popular characters were Colombina, a cheeky servant girl, the ugly and oafish Pulcinella, and Il Capitano who was a swaggering but cowardly soldier.

Brighella

## Easy identification

People recognized these characters by the masks and costumes they wore. Having a recognizable costume made life easier for the actors. It meant that there was no need for them to spend time establishing their character in front of a new audience.

Colombina

Il Capitano Spezzaferro

They could concentrate instead on the dialogue. The actors did not learn their parts from written scripts. A lot of their dialogue was made up on the spot, or improvised.

## A contrived plot

The basic storyline never changed very much. There was always a loving couple. They might be the son and daughter of the two middle-aged characters, who didn't want them to marry. The couple would enlist the help of the clowns and Colombina in changing their fathers' minds. The clowns would set up some ridiculous plan by which the young man could save his girl from some terrible danger. The plan would go disastrously wrong, but then, by some twist in the story, everything would come right in the end. The story wasn't really that important. What the audience enjoyed was all the fun and tomfoolery that went into telling it.

Pantaleone

# Acting and singing

A performance of *The Return of Ulysses* by the Italian composer Claudio Monteverdi

About 400 years ago, a group of friends met at a house in Florence in Italy. They were all interested in music and the theatre, and they wanted to try out a new way of bringing the two together. The idea of introducing songs into theatrical performances was not new. The friends knew that Ancient Greek tragedies had included singing and dancing. The original idea they had was to tell the whole story in music and singing. This was the birth of opera.

## Western opera

The first opera was performed in Florence in 1597. It was called *Dafne*. We don't know much about it because the words, known as the libretto, and the music, or score, have disappeared. A few years later, the Italian composer Claudio Monteverdi was composing operas in which the music cleverly matched the feelings of the characters. These are sometimes known as the first modern operas. This photograph shows a recent production of *The Return of Ulysses* by Monteverdi.

Opera became extremely popular. Big cities, like Venice, had five opera houses, and these were visited by all members of society. A visitor to Italy in 1800 reported that when an opera was to be performed, huge crowds would pour in from the surrounding countryside. They would camp out overnight because the inns were all full. The songs from new operas were known to everyone. They were the pop songs of their day.

An opera stage setting of the 1600s

## Larger than life

Opera does not pretend to be anything like real life. In real life, people don't stand on a grand stage like the one below, and pour out all their thoughts and feelings in song. In an opera, the singers dress and make up to suit the characters they are playing, but they don't try to behave like real people. The characters in an opera are what we call "larger than life".

A scene from *The Marriage of Figaro*, by the Austrian composer Wolfgang Amadeus Mozart

## Making drama into opera

Two favourite operas are *The Marriage of Figaro*, written in 1786 by Mozart, and *The Barber of Seville*, which Rossini wrote in 1816. They are based on two plays by the French dramatist Beaumarchais. The hero of the play, Figaro, is a cheeky, cunning barber who can turn his hand to anything and who knows how to turn everything to his own advantage. Do you think he seems to be boasting about something in this picture of *The Marriage of Figaro*? Beaumarchais' play *The Barber of Seville* was popular, but *The Marriage of Figaro* was a disaster because the French government banned it for several years. They didn't like its criticism of authority. However, the two operas were both huge successes when they first appeared, and they are still widely enjoyed today.

## Sing-speak

Instead of carrying on a normal conversation with someone, try singing it instead. Saying ordinary things such as "Would you like something to drink?" or "I'm going downstairs to turn the television on!" becomes very funny when you sing them. Does your 'opera' have the same rhythm as your speech?

# A famous playwright

William Shakespeare

William Shakespeare was an actor who became a member of a theatre company in London. He certainly learned how to write lines and scenes that would work on stage and how to write parts with specific actors in mind. And he knew what the audiences wanted!

## Subjects for plays

Shakespeare wrote both witty comedies and tragedies, taking his stories from old legends, books written at the time, or even from other people's plays! He also wrote historical plays, some about the kings of England, and some about events in Ancient Greece and Rome. He drew information for these from history, but often altered the facts to make a better story. One of Shakespeare's most bloody tragedies is *Titus Andronicus.* In the old drawing below you can see the queen pleading with Titus to spare the lives of her sons.

It's amazing that such a famous person as the English playwright William Shakespeare should be such a mysterious character. We know he came from Stratford-upon-Avon, a town in the centre of England, and that he married Anne Hathaway. But we don't know much else about his private life. What we do know is that he wrote at least 36 plays, and over 100 poems.

This sketch shows characters in *Titus Andronicus* by William Shakespeare

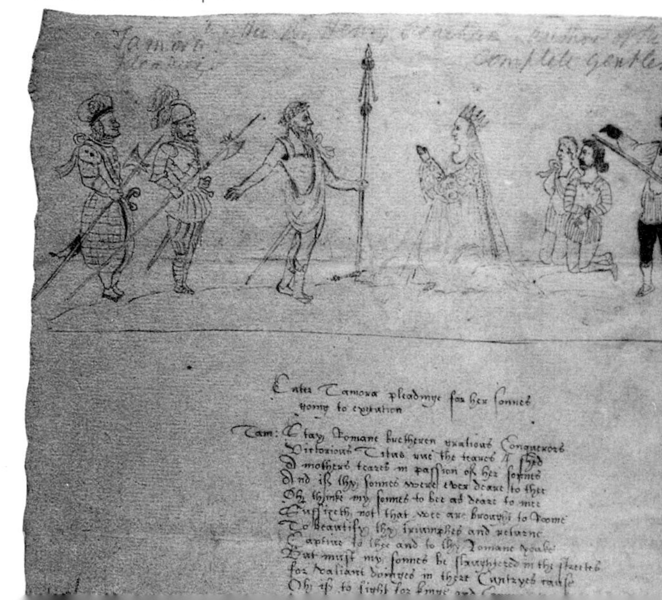

## Varying the pace

Shakespeare's plays are long. They are often cut when they are performed today so that they can be fitted into one evening. But Shakespeare took good care not to bore his audience. In the histories, and even in the tragedies, he included the occasional scene of comedy to lighten the mood. These comic scenes also gave the actors playing the more serious parts a chance to rest and change their costumes.

Another trick that Shakespeare used to keep the interest of the audience was to introduce many changes of scene. For example, his play *The Tempest* starts at sea in a storm. The scene changes quickly to an island, and again to other parts of the island as more characters are introduced. The audience sees four different scenes within the space of a few minutes.

## The Globe Theatre

Many of Shakespeare's plays were performed at the Globe Theatre in London. This many-sided wooden building was built around an open yard. The actors performed on a platform that jutted out into the yard, while the spectators stood or sat in three rows of galleries around the sides. The original theatre burned down in 1613, but you can see from this painting how the Globe would have looked.

The Globe Theatre in London, England, in the early 1600s

# A classical age

Would you enjoy going to see a play based on a classical Greek legend? You probably would if there was lots of action, exciting scenery, and plenty of colourful characters. But Ancient Greek plays weren't like this. They offered no scenery changes, little action and only very strict and serious plots. Do you think this sounds a big boring? Some 2,500 years ago, such plays were very popular.

This picture shows a scene from a play called *Iphigenia*

IPHIGENIE

245

IPHIGENIE.

TRAGEDIE.

ACTE PREMIER.

SCENE I.

AGAMEMNON, ARCAS.

AGAMEMNON.

OUY, c'eſt Agamemnon , c'eſt ton Roy q
t'éveille.
ien, reconnoy la voix qui frappe ton oreille.

ARCAS.

C'eſt vous-meſme , Seigneur ! Quel important beſoi
Vous a fait devancer l'Aurore de ſi loin ?
A peine un foible jour vous éclaire & me guide.
Vos yeux ſeuls & les miens ſont ouverts dans l'Aulide.

## The Greek ideal

In the 1600s in France, classical plays similar to the Greek plays were all the fashion. They were based on rules drawn up by the Ancient Greeks. These rules stated that the plays should be based on a legend or historical event and should make some religious, moral or political point. The plays didn't contain much action. The action took place in one location within a 24-hour span. The real action, especially any violence, death or murder, took place off stage. Messengers appeared from the side of the stage, or the wings, to tell the audience what had happened.

## Jean Racine

The French playwright, Jean Racine, who was born in 1639, wrote a number of classical plays based on the Greek model. This picture shows a scene from a play called *Iphigenia.* The main interest in Racine's plays is not in the plot, it's in seeing what effect the events have on the characters. They are really a kind of subtle psychological drama.

Jean Racine

A performance of *The Imaginary Invalid* by Molière

## Critical comedy

While Racine was writing his tragedies, Molière was giving the French public something to laugh about. Molière was an actor-manager and playwright – he did everything! He travelled around with a troupe of actors putting on comic plays that poked fun at middle-class society. He laughed at pompous or boring people. His later plays were quite outspoken, and sometimes annoyed people. Members of the church, for instance, were upset when, in his plays, Molière made fun of people who pretended to be religious but who were really up to all sorts of mischief.

The grand performance of *The Imaginary Invalid* that you can see in the picture above was given before the king and his court in 1674. Just one year before this occasion, Molière was himself acting in a performance of the play, when he collapsed, and died shortly afterwards.

## The Comédie Française

After Molière died, Europe's first national theatre, the Comédie Française, was formed. It's still going today. You might think from its name that the Comédie Française only perform comedies, but this isn't so. If you ever visit Paris, you could go to this world-famous theatre and see one of the hundreds of plays from the classical or modern repertoire performed there.

# Widening horizons

These people are eagerly trying to get into a theatre in the late 1700s

This sketch shows an audience trying to get into a theatre and grab a seat. What a struggle! On the floor lie women's bonnets and even a couple of shoes. The sketch was drawn in the late 1700s – a time when going to the theatre was a highly popular form of entertainment. Towns and cities were growing in size, and people were looking for amusement in their spare time. In 1700, for example, there were only three theatres in Paris, but just over 20 years later there were over 50. Almost every large town in France boasted at least one theatre during this time. In every country in western Europe there was a similar burst of theatre building.

## Visiting the playhouse

The new theatres came to be known as playhouses and a visit to the playhouse was a fashionable outing. The audience expected to sit in comfort and watch a play full of action and excitement. The new playhouses were roofed and well lit.

In England, London's leading theatre at this time was in Drury Lane. The picture on the opposite page shows the lavish interior of the Drury Lane playhouse in 1808, a theatre which held over 3,500 people. Can you see the enclosed seats which are positioned almost on the stage itself? These boxes are where important or wealthy spectators sat – although the overall view was probably not as good as that in the main part of the theatre.

The interior of the Drury Lane Theatre in London in 1808

## Privacy in a box

The boxes were like small rooms in which a family party could sit together, and enjoy food and drinks in the intervals. They entered the box through a private door. This happy party is occupying a theatre box in the early 1800s. You can see a tray of hot tea which they have brought into the box with them. They certainly have a lot of room in which to stretch their legs! Of course, not everybody was seated in a box. Around the walls of the theatre, rising up in tiers, were balconies or galleries and this is where most of the audience sat.

This etching drawn in 1820 shows a box at the Schouwburg Theatre in Amsterdam, the Netherlands

# CHAPTER TWO

# PERFORMING AROUND THE WORLD

There's a performance somewhere to suit every taste. Enjoy the colour of Japanese Kabuki theatre, or marvel at the scale of an open-air opera. Roar with laughter at a comedy – or cry at the sad ending to a tragedy. Theatre comes in a wonderful variety of forms.

Some plays have remained the same for hundreds of years. People enjoy the unchanging tradition and ceremony of these shows. Other kinds of drama develop over the years, adapting to new ideas and influences.

You'll find plays that are fun, you'll find others that make you think, and yet others that you find weird. Explore the world of theatre!

# All kinds of shows

Buy a theatre ticket and you have a passport to a magical world of make-believe. There's no end to the different kinds of plays you can choose to see. Imagine a play which has no spoken words and which lasts for just over thirty seconds! You'd be watching a play called *Breath* by the English playwright Samuel Beckett. Or you might find yourself in the audience of the Indian dance-drama Kathakali which can take up to eight hours to perform! The play might take place on a tiny stage, or in a huge arena like the one pictured below. The actors might be dressed in specially-made costumes, or they might be acting in everyday clothes. The theatre is full of possibilities.

This performance of *Carmen* was staged in a huge arena

## Happy or sad

What kind of play do you like best? Do you like one that makes you laugh? Do you find that when somebody else laughs, you can't help laughing too? Watch a funny play, a comedy, and you will soon be joining in with the laughter. Tragedies are very different. They are sad stories with unhappy endings.

A performance of Peking Opera

Plays with an action-filled plot are full of excitement and keep you on the edge of your seat. Other dramas are played out at a gentler pace. You may even find you leave the theatre in floods of tears! A sentimental story with a happy ending often makes people cry.

## A good story

So what keeps your attention at the theatre? It could be the costumes, or the actors, or the plot. Just look how absorbed this young audience are in a performance of Peking Opera. The colourful costumes and backcloth have certainly captured their attention, but most of all they are enjoying the story. What will happen next? Will the hero win the day? Everybody enjoys a good story, so wherever you live take every opportunity you can to visit the theatre and see all kinds of drama.

# The spectacle of Kabuki

This woodcut shows the scene inside a Japanese Kabuki theatre

Look at the scene taking place here. Most of the audience have found their seats, and the waiters are serving delicious food – like the plate of fish you can see on the left of the picture. You can almost hear the excited chatter that fills the air. A performance of Japanese Kabuki is about to start. Kabuki is a spectacular show of singing, dancing and acting. Until the actors appear, the stage is hidden by a curtain painted with a traditional Kabuki scene – this one shows a duel.

## The entrance of the actors

The backcloth and scenery for a Kabuki play are elegant but simple so that the audience doesn't pay too much attention to them. All eyes must be on the Kabuki performers from the moment they appear. When the actors are ready to enter, they approach the stage from one of the walkways which cut through the audience. This walkway is known as the hanamichi, or 'flower way'. Kabuki actors dress in lavish

Two Kabuki performers

costumes, richly decorated with embroidery and gold thread. You can see two Kabuki performers in the picture above. Look at the folds of material in the costume on the right. The actor will have to be careful not to trip over his long train!

## Theatre of change

Kabuki has been popular in Japan since the 1600s. One reason is that the actors have always been encouraged to experiment with their roles, presenting them in new ways. In fact Kabuki theatre is always changing. The traditional plays about historical and everyday events are rewritten from time to time to make them more up-to-date for modern audiences.

Machinery helps to keep the action of a Kabuki play moving along quickly. The actors appear and disappear mysteriously through trap doors, and it is quite common to see revolving stages in the Kabuki theatre. These whisk one scene out of sight and immediately put another in its place. Kabuki theatres were fitted with revolving stages as long ago as 1760 – long before such complicated machinery was used anywhere else in the world.

## Larger than life

This is a picture of a famous Kabuki actor, Ennosuke Ichikawa. His costume and long, white hair tell us he is performing the lion dance, which takes place in one of the most popular of the many Kabuki plays. Look at the expression on his face and at his pose. What is he about to do? Perhaps he has 'frozen' – a common pose in Kabuki. This means that the actor stands still for a while holding an especially dramatic moment. Actors also learn to exaggerate their acting, so that their movements are just as eye-catching as their costumes.

The famous Kabuki actor Ennosuke Ichikawa

# Preparing for Kathakali

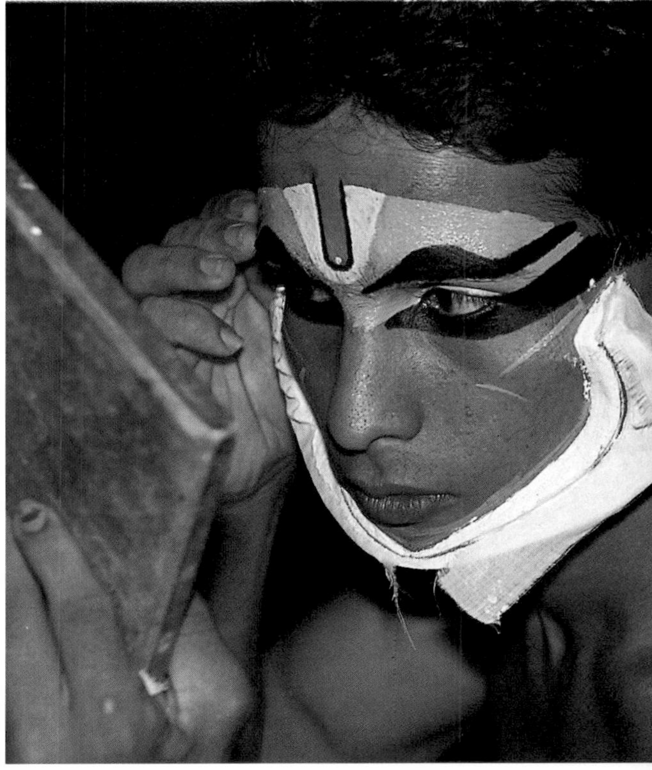

Kathakali is the name given to a mixture of dance, mime and song which is performed by male actors in the state of Kerala in Southern India. It is tremendously popular and is based on legends and myths taken from the Hindu religion. The performers wear lots of make-up and elaborate costumes and head-dresses. The pictures on these pages show Kathakali actors preparing to go on stage. The task of getting ready for a performance obviously takes a long time. In fact it usually takes at least four hours!

This actor is having his make-up applied

## Making up

Gods and demons, heroes and villains – a Kathakali dance-drama centres on strong, imposing figures like these. The audience knows which character is which because of the colour and style of the actors' thick make-up. A green face framed with a white paper border indicates a hero, but a green and red face is worn by a villain. Black make-up is worn by the most evil characters of all.

Kathakali make-up is so thick that the actors' painted faces look like masks. The make-up is put on in stages. If a paper border is added to frame the face, this has to be glued on, and it takes time for the glue to dry. In fact, preparation takes such a long time that many

This Kathakali actor is applying his own make-up

A Kathakali actor puts on his costume

Kathakali actors lie down and relax while their make-up is being put on. But in the end, it's worth spending all that time behind the scenes because the result is so spectacular. Kathakali stages are simple, with no props or scenery, so the arrival of these colourful characters on stage is all the more impressive.

## Costume

The actors usually have to be helped into their costumes. This actor has put on his full skirt. On top of this he adds a decorated shirt and heavy necklaces. Behind him you can see a row of tall, elaborate head-dresses. A head-dress like this is rather heavy, so the actor doesn't put it on until just before he goes on stage. In addition, the actors sometimes wear long silver fingernails to draw attention to their hand movements. Only then is the Kathakali performer ready to go on stage.

# Oberammergau

This print shows a performance of the Oberammergau Passion play in 1870

Have you ever sat and watched a play which lasted for six hours? It's a long time to sit still and watch anything! Yet people from all over the world flock to a small village in the mountains of Bavaria in Germany to do this once every ten years. The village is called Oberammergau, and the event which draws people from so far away is the series of performances from May to September of a religious drama known as a Passion play.

## The first play

Oberammergau's Passion play tells the story of events leading up to the death of Jesus Christ. The play has been performed every ten years since 1634 – except for a few gaps here and there, usually due to war. It began after a dreadful plague which reached Oberammergau in 1633. This plague had already killed hundreds of thousands of people in Europe. The frightened villagers prayed to God to save them – and the plague left the village without a single death. It was a miracle! The grateful villagers decided to stage a religious play every 10 years as a special thank you.

## A cast of hundreds

About 800 people, including a large orchestra and chorus, take part in the play. Where do you think this large cast is found? The actors are not professionals – they are all inhabitants of the village. They train for their parts in the years leading up to the performance. Those who don't get acting parts help with the costumes and scenery. One way or another, everybody gets involved.

The play is made up of 18 different scenes separated by tableaux vivants. These are still-life scenes showing incidents from the Bible story. A tableau vivant of the Last Supper is shown here. The six hours of performance time is broken into two three-hour sections. The actors wear no make-up or wigs, but they make a great effort to grow their hair and beards to the right style for the time of Christ. For months before each performance, the village is full of people with long hair and beards! Such dedication shows that the Oberammergau Passion play is a very special event.

A tableau vivant of the Last Supper

# Stories of the past

The Oberammergau Passion play which you read about on the previous pages is the oldest community play still performed. But community plays involving local people are staged in other places, too, although they are not always to do with religion. They might be staged to celebrate an important occasion or to illustrate a colourful local legend. What is important is that they bring people together and keep alive stories which may be hundreds, and perhaps thousands, of years old.

These plays are not always written down. Very often they will have been passed down by word of mouth from generation to generation. This storyteller is performing to an audience in the Sudan. He is keeping the local people in touch with the ancient myths and legends from their past.

This Sudanese storyteller has collected an eager audience

These actors are performing for a wedding party in southern India

## Bringing a story alive

Myths and legends provide a rich source of material for short plays or sketches. And when storytellers act out the story themselves or, even better, with other performers, the story becomes a dramatic performance. It takes on a new form.

The performers you can see in the picture on the right are entertaining a crowd at a wedding in southern India. The weather is so hot that they are sheltering in the cool shade provided by a group of trees. The actors are wearing bells round their ankles so that every movement is accompanied by a lively jingle. What do you think is going on? It looks as if they are acting a violent scene, with the man on the ground about to be beaten. But the actors' expressions are not exactly fierce. They are clearly enjoying themselves – and so are the audience. It is fun to watch a well-known story brought to life in this way.

## Act your own stories

Think of the stories you listened to when you were younger. You may have heard them at home, or at school, or maybe on the radio or television. Do you think you could make a play out of one of them? Could you do this with a group of friends?

You'll need to collect a few props. If your story includes animal characters, you will need some masks. If you can't find any, why not make some eye masks from egg boxes like the ones shown here. If you choose well-known stories, you won't need to write down the words. Everyone will know more or less what is supposed to happen next.

# Repertory

Imagine a troupe of actors is visiting you at home! First you would all need to get together to decide where they would set up their stage, and which play they would perform. This is what used to happen hundreds of years ago when groups of Chinese actors were summoned to perform at a rich landowner's house. They didn't know until they arrived which play they were going to put on. The landowner made the choice, and, of course, he always requested one of his favourites. The travelling actors knew dozens of different plays and could perform any of them on request. The plays they knew made up their repertory.

The interior of the RSC's theatre in Stratford-upon-Avon, England

## Rep and stock

Since then, repertory, or rep, has come to have two different meanings. It can refer to the collection of plays that a group of actors know and can fit into a changing programme. It can also mean a group of actors who learn a play and perform it for a week or two, before going on to a new play. The actors stay together as a group and work in a particular theatre. Another name for this kind of repertory is 'stock theatre'.

## The Royal Shakespeare Company

The repertory system is widely used in Europe. One of the most famous repertory groups in the world is the Royal Shakespeare Company, based in the famous theatre shown here at Stratford-upon-Avon in England. They also perform at the Barbican theatre in London. The Royal Shakespeare Company, or RSC, specializes in performing plays by playwrights of the 1500s and 1600s, especially those written by the English playwright William Shakespeare. On the right you can see members of the RSC performing one of Shakespeare's plays, *The Comedy of Errors.*

## The advantage of rep

Many actors prefer to work in rep. They get the chance to play a range of parts in many different types of play and they come to know the strengths and weaknesses of the actors they are working with. In addition to this, they can make sure they don't always play the same kind of part, which is known as being typecast. Some actors spend months or even years playing the same part night after night, and they risk going stale. In rep, the performers don't go stale – they don't have a chance to.

Members of the RSC performing *The Comedy of Errors* by William Shakespeare

# Interpreting great plays

What makes a play great? You could say it's one that goes on being popular with audiences for years and years. One play in London, *The Mousetrap* by Agatha Christie, has run continuously since 1952! There's something in a great play that interests everyone, regardless of who they are or where they live. They will still be popular with your grandchildren, no matter how much fashions change in the meantime!

## Freedom in performance

Some popular plays follow traditions that are hundreds of years old, but which still please audiences today. Other great plays can be put on without such close attention to tradition. The words are written down, so we know what the characters are supposed to say. But there are no set rules about what the actors should wear, or what dramatic gestures they should make, or how the scenery should look. Each production of these kinds of play can become a completely new experience because the scenery, the costumes and the style of acting can vary each time. This often means that you discover something new about the play every time you see a different performance of it.

## Shakespeare's greatness

Most people would agree that the English writer, Shakespeare was one of the world's greatest playwrights. From the 1600s, when Shakespeare wrote his plays, they have been constantly performed throughout the world, and in many different forms. Films, music, operas and many, many books have been based on his plays and the characters in them.

These actors are rehearsing *Romeo and Juliet* on a bomb site

Look at these pictures of Shakespearean productions. You'll see that they are all very different. The black-and-white photograph shows some students rehearsing the play, *Romeo and Juliet.* Their costumes look old-fashioned so you get the impression that the play took place a long time ago. But the students are not acting on stage. They are acting on a bomb site! The audience of three little boys is clearly wondering what's going to happen next.

The picture on the right shows a performance of *A Midsummer Night's Dream.* This performance did not take

A scene from a production of *The Winter's Tale* by William Shakespeare

An open-air performance of *A Midsummer Night's Dream* in London, England

place in a theatre either, but out in the open air. The masks and costumes look fantastic, to match the magical atmosphere of the play. In the centre, the man holding a cloud of balloons is Autolycus, a character in *The Winter's Tale.* Autolycus is a rascal, a trickster and a pickpocket. These pictures show you that Shakespeare's plays can be performed in a variety of styles and still be popular. That must be a sign of great writing!

# Peking Opera

About 2,000 years ago, China was a wealthy empire bordered to the north by the mountains of Mongolia. Fierce tribes came down to plunder Chinese villages and steal anything valuable that they could find. They helped themselves to money and food and, sometimes, they took Chinese villagers as slaves. The Great Wall of China was built to stop these raids, but it was not completely successful for raiders still managed to cross the wall.

*Beauty*, one of the most popular plays in Chinese theatre, is set against this background of war and strife. It is based on a true story and was written at least 200 years ago. You can see a scene from *Beauty* in the picture above. Beauty was a princess who was kidnapped by Mongolian raiders. In spite of many adventures and sufferings, she stayed loyal to China and in the end died for her country. In the play, there is plenty of scope for song, dance and, in the battle scenes, there are even acrobatics.

A performance of the Peking Opera, *Beauty*

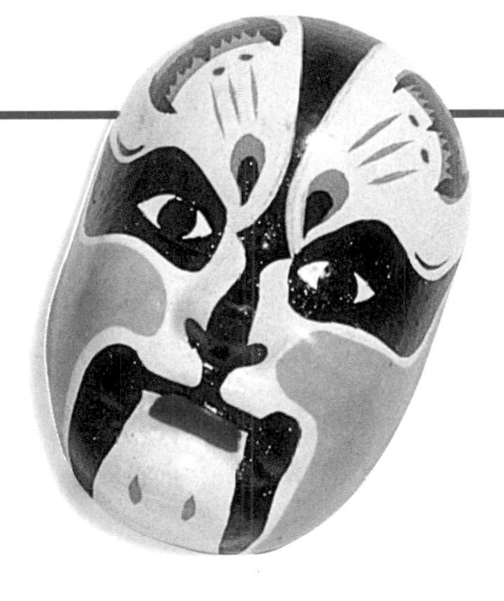

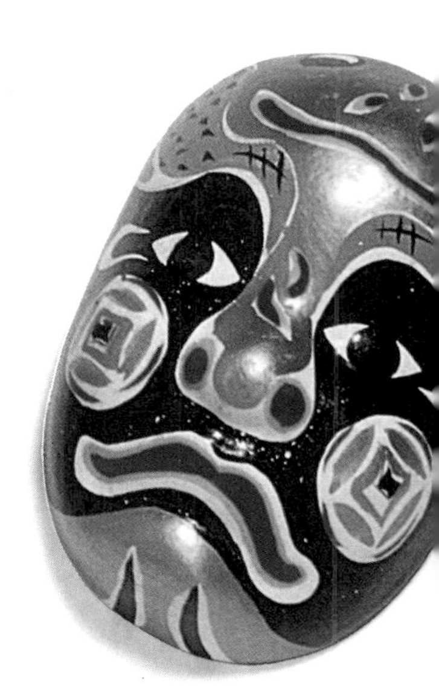

## Actors' theatre

A Chinese play like *Beauty* which combines song, dance and drama is known as Peking Opera, or, by its Chinese name, ching hsi. Peking Opera is different from western opera because the plays are performed without fixed pieces of scenery. Painted banners and boards are carried onto the stage by stagehands to represent the actors' surroundings. They might carry blue silk banners to represent water, or place a chair on stage to represent a hill. Because the scenery is so simple, the audience relies on the skill of the actors to describe the action. Their movements and facial expressions are the most important part of the drama, which is why it is called actors' theatre.

Just because there is little scenery, Peking Opera is no less spectacular to watch than western opera. The actors dress in magnificent costumes and wear thick, greasepaint make-up. The costumes and the colours of the face paint tell the audience which character is which. Pheasant feathers and specially-coloured flags are worn by the actors playing the important characters. Red face paint indicates a loyal and courageous character. And, unusually, black is worn by a good person, while white indicates a wicked character. Orange and grey are worn by elderly characters.

These miniature masks show traditional Peking Opera make-up

You can see a vividly made-up Peking Opera performer here. The three miniature masks show other traditional forms of Peking Opera make-up.

This Peking Opera performer wears striking make-up

# Street theatre

Street performers in London, England

What is the first thing you notice about the picture below? It's probably the fact that the actors are not performing on a stage, but out in the open. They are wearing their own clothes – not special costumes – and have very few props. You can just see a basket and a rattle. In fact, the scene isn't so unusual. Most actors can work wherever there is an open space – from passageways and streets to market places and courtyards. The stage area is formed by the audience which gathers around them.

These actors are performing in a street in the San Blas islands, off the coast of Panama

## Attracting attention

Street actors bring entertainment to people who might never go to a theatre. This means that the actors have to work really hard to grab the attention of passers-by, and persuade them to stop and watch! These four performers are definitely eye-catching! Do you think you would stop to watch their act? Their appearance probably drew in a large crowd at Covent Garden in London.

Street theatre is usually made up of short, simple pieces, so that it is easy for newcomers to see what is going on. The photographers have certainly planned an act, because they have brought their costumes and their cameras with them. But although most street performers prepare an outline of the plot, they are also prepared to improvise. Improvisation is the art of making things up as you go along. It's quite a skill! The actors have to react quickly to the audience, sometimes involving them in the action or making them part of the joke.

This Parisian street performer is preparing for her act

## Dressing in the street

Performing on the street means you need to carry with you everything you are likely to need. This might be very little. But sometimes street performers need more equipment. This Parisian street performer has two large bags to carry all her equipment. In the first picture, you can see that make-up and props have been arranged against some park railings where the performer is preparing for her show. She has even brought along a tape recorder to provide background music for her act.

In the second picture she has begun to perform, and has quickly collected an audience. This audience probably began to gather round out of curiosity while she was preparing her costume and make-up. They are getting an unusual peep behind the scenes. Do you think this adds to the excitement of the performance? Anything can happen in street drama, so stop and watch next time you notice some street theatre in action.

A street performer in Paris, France

# The masked dancers of Asia

That part of south-east Asia which now makes up the countries of Thailand, Kampuchea and Vietnam, was once the battleground of two rival empires, the Thais and the Khmers. In 1431, the Thais overran the Khmers and the two empires became one, and that's probably when the famous masked dance-dramas of this region developed.

## Khmer dance-dramas

The dance-dramas of the Khmers may have started with the custom of dancing in the imperial palace to encourage rainfall and good crops. By about 1400, these dances had developed into dramas called lakhon khol which told exciting and often very complicated stories.

In the days of the Khmer empire, several hundred dancers and musicians were employed at the imperial court. The dancers, all women, mimed the story while a hidden chorus, accompanied by musicians, sang the words. Some of the stories were drawn from the Ramayana, the collection of legends of the Hindu religion. Others were based on Khmer legends. In the days of the Khmer empire, performances often lasted for many hours. Today, any performances you may see won't last so long. They are usually made up of a number of short dances which are taken from different plays.

Khon dancers from Thailand

movements of the dancers and the patterns their feet make on the stage all have special meanings. The dancers move in rather an unusual way. In fact, they move more like puppets than living people, gliding smoothly from side to side across the stage. They don't move backwards or forwards to use its full depth. It may be that, long ago, the Khmer dances began as shadow-puppet shows, which would explain how this style of dancing came about.

## Tradition in Thailand

The dance-dramas of Thailand which are traditionally, though not always, performed in masks are known as khon. Unlike the lakhon khol, they are performed by both male and female dancers wearing costumes made from richly patterned and embroidered materials. The khon are not unlike the dramas of the Khmer empire. The masks, the stories and the movements of the dancers are all similar. In fact, the Thai army probably saw performances of Khmer drama when they invaded the Khmer court, and then copied them.

## Unchanging tradition

Khon dance-dramas have remained unchanged for hundreds of years because the stories are drawn from traditional myths and legends. The

# Plays with a message

This actor is performing for a community development group in Tanzania

Plays are not always written just to entertain a theatre audience. Sometimes, a writer wants to send a clear message to the world. This message often deals with something that is extremely important to the writer – religion or politics, for example.

## Theatre for development

Sometimes a play is written specifically to teach people something. It might, for example, show parents how to set up and run a children's play-group. Since the 1950s, this form of educational theatre has become quite common in countries like Africa and India. It is known as theatre for development. People have found that putting on an interesting play is a much more effective way to teach others about important subjects like health care than just talking to them. The man shown above is an actor with a theatre for development group working in Tanzania. Similar acting groups also work in England, where they tour schools performing educational plays to young children. Their plays spread important messages such as the need for road safety or the dangers of drugs.

Henrik Ibsen

## The power of the playwright

Theatre has always been used to express strongly-held views. These could be a protest against the government of the day, or support for a religious point of view. One of the most famous playwrights to write about such important issues in the form of drama was a Norwegian called Henrik Ibsen.

Ibsen wrote scripts about the kinds of problem which affect the lives of ordinary people, like bad luck and unhappiness.

In the 1900s, his plays became successful throughout Europe and America, and his ideas have had a worldwide influence ever since. Ibsen urged the actors in his plays to act in a down-to-earth manner to suit the theme of his plot. This method of acting is called naturalistic acting – you can read more about it on page 134.

## Teaching your audience

What do you think is the best way to use drama to teach your audience something? Imagine you want to convince them that the best way to wash up is with a particular kind of washing-up brush. You might try using a cloth, but you'd pretend not to like getting wet hands. You could show how a scourer might scratch the pan. You could use twigs or sand, but they wouldn't do a good job. You'd need to show lots of alternatives, but find something wrong with all of them! Finally, you try the wonder brush and show how well it works to persuade your audience that it's the best way to wash up! Try using this method to send other kinds of messages.

Two scenes showing San Blas islanders performing a historical drama

# The power of drama

These pictures show people from the islands of San Blas performing a play. It is a re-telling of an important event in their history, marking a revolution in 1925 when the islanders rebelled against the government of Panama because they wanted to rule the islands themselves. Many people were killed, so the San Blas people want to remember the event, in the hope that it will never happen again. They perform the play as a powerful reminder.

## The strength of the theatre

Political drama like this can be very persuasive. It is a particularly good way of getting a message across. That's why governments and rulers often take great interest in what happens in their local theatres. In the past, governments have even banned plays which they thought were disruptive and dangerous. Some still do. Other governments give money to theatre companies who put on plays they approve of. This is what happened in Russia from the 1920s to the 1980s. The result was that most of the plays seen by Russian audiences during those years showed the government as efficient and fair. This was a one-sided view that wasn't always true! We call writing that only presents one point of view like this, propaganda.

Propaganda isn't always a bad thing. Many countries throughout the world now hold environmental weeks to spread ideas about the ways in which people can help save the planet. Drama can play an important part in such events. This illustration shows performers in the Solomon Islands. They are wearing giant fish-shaped costumes to perform a dance-drama during an environmental week held there in 1990. Can you think what they were trying to do? They wanted to use the event to draw attention to over-fishing in their seas. They used a light-hearted form of propaganda to put across a serious message.

# The extravagance of opera

This opera is taking place in a huge arena at Verona, Italy

Just look at the number of people involved in the production shown here. You would have a difficult job to count everybody. Apart from those on stage, there's a large orchestra sitting in the pit which divides the stage from the audience. This spectacular form of theatre is called opera, and it draws huge audiences into theatres and amphitheatres in countries all over the world.

Many operas are performed on a large scale. The cast of actors, dancers and singers, all dressed in beautiful costumes, may number more than 100 people. As you can imagine, the stage sets have to be huge to make room for this many people. And don't forget all the people you can't see – those working behind the scenes. Altogether, hundreds of people may be involved in a single operatic production.

## Performing an opera

Opera is a combination of singing and acting. It's a combination that takes a lot of skill – not all singers can act, and not all actors can sing – so operatic performers usually train for a long time. When you're singing you can't do all the things you can do when you're just acting. You can't dash across the stage or get involved in a sword fight.

Many opera singers start their career by singing in the chorus until, finally, they are lucky enough to be given a small part of their own, a solo. Some performers go on to sing the principal parts, and just a few reach fame and fortune. Have you heard of New Zealand's Kiri Te Kanawa, Jamaica's Willard White or Grace Bumbry from the United States of America? They are some of the most famous principal opera singers in the world. This picture shows Grace Bumbry preparing for a performance in her dressing room. Principal singers often wear fabulous costumes so that the audience definitely knows who is the star!

## Elephants on stage

This Italian newspaper captures something of the grand scale of the 1938 performance of an opera called *Aida*. *Aida* was written in the 1800s by the Italian composer Giuseppe Verdi. It is set in Ancient Egypt, and contains many scenes involving large crowds. The 1938 performance was actually staged in Egypt, with real elephants making an appearance. But even the huge elephants were dwarfed by the enormous Egyptian temples around them! This must have been a memorable evening for the audience – as well as for the cast.

The American opera singer Grace Bumbry

This newspaper reviewed a performance of *Aida* which took place in 1902

# Singing and dancing

Roll up! Roll up! All the fun of the fair! Form a queue and ride the horses on the carousel! Dim the lights and turn up the music ... this is the place to be! But wait a minute – don't be fooled. The funfair ride in the picture below isn't part of a real fair at all – it was made especially for the stage. It forms part of the background scenery, or set, for a lively stage show called *Carousel.*

## The fun of a musical

You can see that the sets for this kind of show are just as lavish as those built for operas. In fact, like operas, these stage productions also contain a lot of singing – as well as speaking. We call a show like *Carousel*, a musical.

Musicals are energetic, often humorous shows which feature an orchestra, and a large cast of singers and dancers. There are often complicated scene changes and lots of special effects – all this as well as acting! The music is lighter than opera music, and has a jolly, rhythmic beat. If you go to watch a musical you will soon be tapping your feet, and enjoying the sight of the stage sets and costumes. A good musical is a feast for the eyes as well as the ears.

The stage set for the musical *Carousel*

Costumed performers from *Starlight Express* by the English composer Andrew Lloyd Webber

## Actors or trains?

This picture shows four performers from a popular British musical called *Starlight Express*. Have you noticed that they are wearing roller skates? That's because they are pretending to be trains, and whizzing around the stage on wheels helps the audience to imagine speeding trains. The actors even skate over the heads of the audience on specially-constructed pathways! Look how their costumes have been designed to allow them to move about freely as they skate, sing and act, all at the same time. What a performance!

## Operettas

Another form of musical theatre is an operetta. Operettas are similar to musicals, telling an entertaining story through spoken dialogue, singing and dancing. Many operettas were written in the 1800s by a pair of British musicians now widely known by their surnames, Gilbert and Sullivan. Their operettas are still performed all over the world. This poster is advertising a Japanese production of a Gilbert and Sullivan operetta called *The Mikado*.

This Japanese poster is advertising Gilbert and Sullivan's operetta, *The Mikado*

# Children's theatre in Russia

A performance by the Obraztsov puppet theatre, Moscow

Russian children are lucky! They have lots of plays which are staged especially for them. For more than eighty years, companies specializing in children's theatre have presented all kinds of plays in all the languages of the former Soviet Union. There are fairy tales, classics, historical dramas, comedies and musicals, often including dance and acrobatics. This picture shows a scene in a performance by a popular puppet theatre based in Moscow in Russia.

## Watch and learn

The younger children can enjoy shows which offer straightforward entertainment and fun, while for older children, the experience can be more educational.

The plays they have studied in school are brought to life on stage. Afterwards, they discuss the play in class. It's an interesting way to learn!

## A fishy tale

Russia has a wonderful store of folk tales. Have you ever heard the story of the *Fisherman and the Goldfish*? It was written by the Russian writer and dramatist Alexander Pushkin, who is pictured here. His story is a popular subject for children's plays in Russia. A poor old fisherman and his wife live in a tumbledown cottage by the sea. One day, the fisherman catches a goldfish. The goldfish pleads with the fisherman to put him back in the sea, promising to give the fisherman whatever he asks for. So the kind-hearted fisherman puts the goldfish back in the sea, and goes home to tell his wife what has happened.

The old woman grumbles that the fisherman did not ask for something as a reward. "Go back and ask for a new washtub," she orders. "Ours is cracked and falling to pieces." So the old man returns to the sea, and humbly asks the goldfish for a new washtub. When he gets home, there it is!

Do you think that makes his wife happy? No! She wants a new house, rich clothes, and lots of servants. Each wish is granted. She even becomes queen!

But then the woman goes too far. She demands that she become mistress of all the seas, with the goldfish as her servant. The fisherman relays the demand. The goldfish just swishes its tail in response. When the old man gets home, he finds the palace, the servants, the finery all gone. There is his tumbledown cottage, and on the doorstep sits his wife, with her old washtub by her side.

Alexander Pushkin

## Make your own rod puppets

Do you like this story? If you were producing it on stage, how would you present it? How do you think the goldfish would be made to talk? How would you show the old woman's greedy lifestyle? Turn to page 113 to find an idea for a toy theatre project you can make at home. You might like to adapt the theatre to suit this story. Use the ideas shown to make rod puppet characters for the goldfish, and for the fisherman and his wife. Just draw the characters on card, cut them out and attach them to sticks with sticky tape.

# Fun and laughter

Just look at this line-up of characters! What are they doing? The arrival of the man on the right appears to have put all the other characters into a state of shock. He certainly has a wicked glare. But what is happening at the other end of the line? Is the woman really being strangled? Do you think the play is meant to be frightening, or is it a comedy? Look again at the ridiculous posturing of the actors and at the expressions on their faces. The scene looks exaggerated and rather fun. It is in fact a scene from a comedy play known as a farce. The farce is called *Thark.*

## A sense of humour

What makes you laugh? Is it practical jokes with lots of action, like someone slipping on a banana skin – or someone clowning around? Maybe you prefer verbal humour – jokes created by using a word in an unexpected way. We smile and laugh for so many different reasons, and everybody has a different sense of humour. In Hindu drama, the monkey-god Hanuman plays all sorts of fierce tricks on humans. Some people think these tricks are cruel, while others think they are funny.

These actors are performing in a comedy called *Thark*, by Ben Travers

On the other hand, humour in Japan is very gentle. Have you heard the joke about the king of the monkeys who asked his servants to capture the reflection of the moon? When, after enormous difficulty, one of the monkeys managed to get the moon clearly reflected in the water, he asked the king what he was going to do with it. "Mm," said the king, "I hadn't thought about that."

## Farce

In a farce, the characters on stage find themselves in awkward or ridiculous situations. They are desperate not to be discovered. They hide behind doors on stage, or in cupboards, or run upstairs. They pretend to be someone else. They dash about the stage trying not to be seen by the people they don't want to meet. But of course, they end up bumping into all the wrong people, the truth comes out, and everything comes right in the end. Look at the scene from *It Runs in the Family*. The old man looks a little too sprightly to be in a wheelchair, so he is probably only pretending to be an invalid.

## Happy laughter

Laughter expresses happiness. When you're happy, you feel lively and energetic – the two seem to go together. Comic actors often carry us along with their energy. They put such fun and happiness into their acts that the audience soon catches the mood.

A scene from a farce called *It Runs in the Family*, by Ray Cooney

Look at this performer in the Trinidad Tent Theatre. He is certainly enjoying his act – you can almost hear him encouraging the spectators to share his joke. A good comedy is fun for everyone.

An actor in the Trinidad Tent Theatre

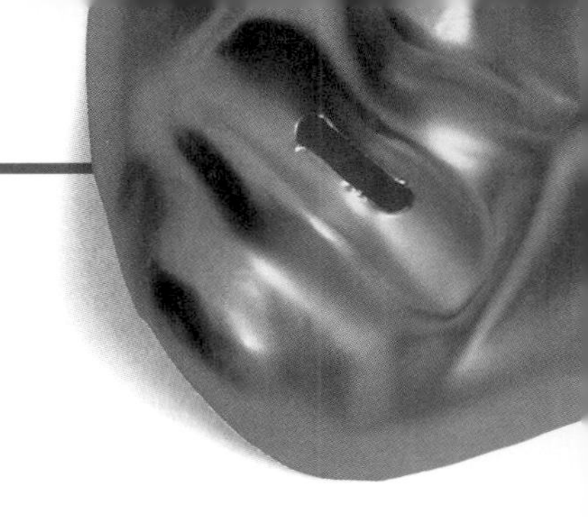

# A sad world

This engraving shows an English tragedy

Have you ever been to a play which has made you cry? It seems odd that anyone should want to go to the theatre to watch a sad play. But that's just what happens sometimes. Some plays are so sad, they make everyone in the audience feel unhappy. These plays are usually called tragedies.

## What is tragedy?

The Ancient Greeks believed that tragedy was the highest form of art. Greek tragedy had a set form and a set style. Now we think of tragedy as the direct opposite of comedy – something sad as opposed to something funny.

If you were watching the play shown in the picture above, you'd know it was a tragedy. Just look at the number of bodies on the stage! With so many deaths involved, it might be a tragedy acted in an exaggerated way, called melodrama. You can read more about melodrama on page 132.

Federico Garcia Lorca

## The sad side of life

Not all tragedies end with a stage strewn with bodies. Some deal with the problems of ordinary people who are unhappy in their ordinary lives. They might be angry, depressed or jealous, or they might have been involved in a crime.

This picture shows a Spanish playwright called Federico Garcia Lorca. Lorca's tragedies about everyday peasant life in Spain became famous. His plays are all about characters who are instantly recognizable to the audience, who easily understand their suffering. Sadly, Garcia Lorca himself had a tragic death – when he was murdered in the Spanish Civil War in 1936.

## An impossible dream

The American playwright Arthur Miller wrote a famous play called *Death of a Salesman.* In this play, an ageing salesman called Willy Loman comes to realize that all his efforts to lead a successful life have failed. In the end, he commits suicide, hoping that his two sons, Biff and Happy, will benefit from a life insurance policy. It is a very sad play. A critic at the first performance wrote that the people in the audience were so moved that they sobbed loudly into their handkerchiefs.

## Make yourself miserable

When they are on stage, actors have to forget about their own lives and their own problems. They need to think themselves into the character they are playing. The audience must be able to believe in that character as a real person. If actors have to cry on stage, they must cry convincingly.

Can you make yourself cry? Think of something really sad. Blink several times. Try sniffing and catching your breath. Consciously try to squeeze some tears out of your eyes. Does it work?

A scene from *Death of a Salesman*, by Arthur Miller

# Theatre of the absurd

These actors are performing in *Endgame*, by the Irish playwright Samuel Beckett

What do you think is going on here? A man and a woman are peering out of two dustbins! How did they manage to get into them? The bins are probably placed over trap doors in the stage floor, so that the actors can climb up into them from below. The whole effect is really unexpected – in fact, this form of stage play has a very appropriate name. It is known as theatre of the absurd.

## Funny or serious?

Theatre of the absurd developed in the 1940s and 1950s. Some playwrights at this time felt that life had become empty and impossible and the only way to treat it was to take ordinary things and turn them upside-down. The result was often amusing, though it wasn't always meant to be. The play in which two people live in dustbins is called *Endgame*. It was written by an Irish playwright called Samuel Beckett. He wrote it to illustrate the hopeless, trapped feeling he had about life.

## The waiting game

Samuel Beckett wrote some of his plays in French and some in English. His play

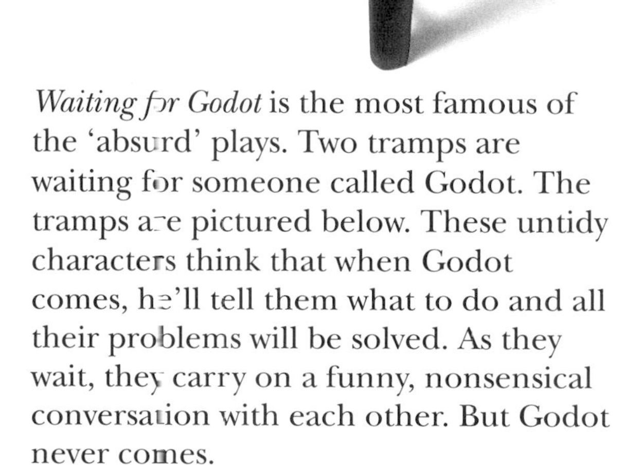

*Waiting for Godot* is the most famous of the 'absurd' plays. Two tramps are waiting for someone called Godot. The tramps are pictured below. These untidy characters think that when Godot comes, he'll tell them what to do and all their problems will be solved. As they wait, they carry on a funny, nonsensical conversation with each other. But Godot never comes.

Do you think you would enjoy *Waiting for Godot*? When it was first performed in London, many of the audience walked out, dismissing the play as rubbish! However, it soon became very popular and today it is often performed.

A scene from *Waiting for Godot*, by Samuel Beckett

## Chairs, chairs and more chairs

Another playwright known for absurd drama is a French writer called Eugène Ionesco. He has written a number of plays that seem absolutely ridiculous. Some of them have strange titles such as *The Bald Prima Donna*, or *Rhinoceros.* They are full of crazy conversations, long silences and misunderstandings. Some of the dialogue is just nonsense language.

In another play by Ionesco, called *The Chairs,* the main characters are an old man and woman in their nineties. One by one, visitors arrive, but these visitors are invisible. The old couple fetch a chair for each new arrival, so that in the end, the stage is covered with chairs, and the old people can't move. Now that is absurd! Then a real visitor arrives, but he is deaf and dumb. He can't speak properly, or do anything more than grunt and groan. Absurd drama often has a sad twist.

# On tour

Actors do not only travel within their own countries. Many acting troupes now go on overseas tours, introducing the world's finest performances and productions to new audiences. Air travel means that international theatre tours are easier than ever before. But even when the only way to travel overseas was by ship, troupes of actors were still taking their plays from one continent to another.

This Nigerian acting troupe have brought their show to England

The first American tour by a European theatrical company took place nearly 250 years ago, in 1752! By the 1850s, leading actors from Europe and North America were crossing the Atlantic by steamship. And today, acting troupes regularly travel out of South America, India and Africa. This picture shows a Nigerian performing arts company who took their show to England.

## The value of a tour

A tour like the one made by the Nigerian company is valuable in a number of ways. This particular show is based on popular traditions which are widely known to the Tiv people in Nigeria. The huge puppets are used in performances which tell people about life in their part of Nigeria. Singers, accompanied by musicians, back the puppet actors. It is a fun-packed and lively show, with a new message for audiences abroad.

These Peking Opera performers are appearing in Thailand

## The spread of Chinese drama

Overseas tours are also important in spreading theatrical ideas. Few people in the western world had ever seen Chinese acting until about 1930. Then a Chinese producer called Qi Rushan teamed up with a group led by a famous Chinese actor, Mei Lanfang, in a world tour. You can read more about Mei Lanfang on page 141.

Mei Lanfang's group performed traditional Chinese plays to audiences in Japan, the United States of America, western Europe and Russia. Today Chinese theatre groups continue to travel around the world – the Chinese performers in the picture above are appearing in Thailand.

Mei Lanfang's overseas tour was the start of a wide interest in Asian drama. One important effect of this was that many stage directors and playwrights in the West, like Bertolt Brecht in Germany, began to try out Chinese styles of acting in their own shows. In fact, Brecht's form of theatre became very influential in Europe, and later in Africa and Asia as well. Asian theatre had influenced a European playwright who added his own ideas and who then became important in Asia. Lanfang's tour had proved a valuable opportunity for the exchange of ideas about theatre.

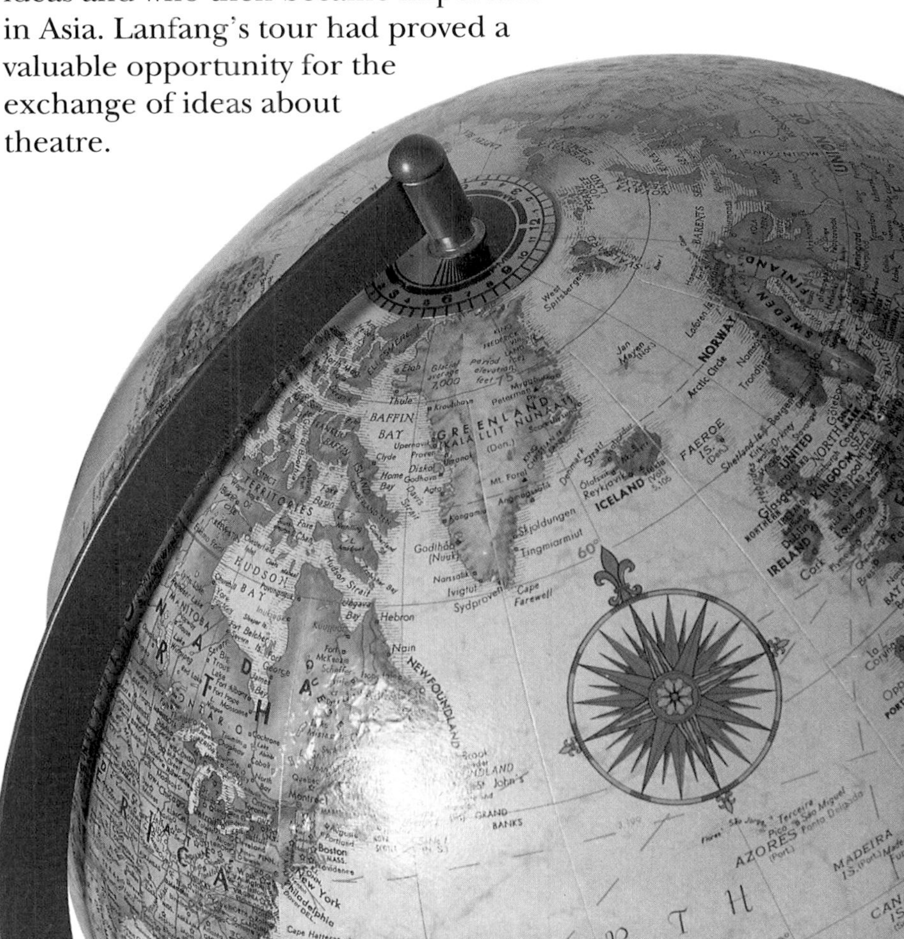

# CHAPTER THREE

# THEATRE OF COLOUR AND SPECTACLE

In this chapter you can read about drama with a difference! Not all plays are acted out in a theatre. Some performances are staged in the open air, in the street or even in a huge tent. You'll read about the fun of carnival and see clowns fooling around. You'll also read about the amazing world of pantomime, and learn how theatre can teach us about the past.

And discover a wonderful world of small-scale theatre in which the actors are puppets. It's easy to forget just how skilled a puppeteer has to be to make a puppet move properly. Later, try this for yourself, by making and operating your own puppets.

# Masques

This is a detail from a painting of Sir Henry Unton by an unknown English artist

How do you usually celebrate a special day such as your birthday? If you're lucky, you might be able to invite a few close friends to a party, with delicious food and exciting games thrown in. However, imagine how big your party would be if you were to invite everyone who lives in your neighbourhood! Some 2,500 years ago, the members of the Chinese imperial court often celebrated special events with a party as large as this. There was a huge meal called a banquet, followed by a performance from entertainers wearing costumes and masks. These extravagant parties were called masques.

## Singing and dancing

Masques also became popular in the royal courts of Europe in the 1500s and 1600s. Members of the court would compete with each other to put on the most extravagant and sumptuous show as a sign of wealth. Singers, masked dancers, and actors were employed to perform mimes, poems and tableaux. A tableau was a scene from history portrayed by a group of actors frozen, silent and motionless, in a pose. You can see a court masque taking place in this picture. Fireworks sometimes lit up the sky, and there was always a grand ball as a finale.

## Scenery and costume

The stage setting or scenery for a masque was usually specially made on a grand scale and was often designed by a well-known architect of the time. In the 1500s, an Italian architect called Bernardo Buontalenti designed very clever pieces of machinery which were used to move scenery quickly on and off stage, or which allowed the performers to appear on stage or disappear suddenly.

Two designs for masque costumes by Inigo Jones

In 1612, an English architect called Inigo Jones even designed a new royal palace especially as a setting for masques. It was called Whitehall. We know a good deal about Inigo Jones's masques because many of the drawings in which he sketched out his ideas for scenery and costumes still exist.

## The masque dies

Originally, poems and speeches formed the main part of each masque. But it was really action and spectacle that the audiences wanted, and gradually most of the words were dropped. Instead, music became a more important part of the celebration, with instruments such as the lute providing a gentle background noise. As opera became more popular in the 1600s, fewer masques were performed. Eventually, the original form of the masque died out altogether, but its influence can still be seen in the machines and moveable scenery used in theatres today.

An English lute

# The pageant

'The Triumph of Isabella, Brussels' was painted in 1615 by Denis van Alsloot

Hundreds of years ago, huge celebrations were staged in honour of some special event, such as the king's entry into a city, or a royal coronation or a grand wedding. These celebrations were called pageants. A pageant consisted of a set of dramatic scenes performed by actors as they rode through the streets on richly decorated carts. Each scene was a short play in itself. The whole town or village would line the streets to enjoy the pageant as it passed by. A pageant could be a kind of religious procession, too. In Europe, the pageant often depicted stories from the Bible, such as the building of Noah's Ark or the adventure of Jonah and the Whale.

## Plays in procession

The picture above shows a pageant which took place in the 1600s in Brussels, the capital of Belgium. You can see that the carts were all decorated differently, to suit each story to be performed. Of course, pageants took place long before the invention of engines, so the carts were pulled by teams of horses. Some carts were built in three tiers, one on top of the other. In the 1600s, European towns had very narrow and crowded streets. Just think how difficult it must have been to manoeuvre these awkwardly-shaped structures around these streets.

When the pageant reached an open space, each cart stopped and the actors on it performed their scene in front of the crowd that soon gathered. Then the procession moved on until the next cart was in place to entertain the crowd with a new scene. The actors were ordinary craftspeople rather than professional actors. There were carpenters, painters, goldsmiths and stonemasons. Often, each group of craftspeople would be responsible for one scene. For example, the carpenters might act out the Noah's Ark scene, while the painters performed the building of King Solomon's temple.

## Pageants today

Pageant processions still take place in some parts of the world. One of the largest happens once a year in India to mark an important festival in the Hindu religion – the birthday of the Hindu god Jagannatha. On this day, huge carts called juggernauts are dragged through the streets to the local Hindu temples.

You can see a juggernaut in the picture on the right. Look how tiny the waiting crowds appear alongside this massive, moving platform! The juggernauts have 16 wheels and are decorated with paintings and carvings of Hindu gods. The musicians and dancers perform on these to the watching crowds.

This cart is used in India to celebrate the birthday of Jagannatha, a Hindu god

## Make a pageant cart

You can make a pageant cart of your own. Start with a cardboard box and fix some wheels to the base. These don't have to be real wheels – cut-out ones will look just as good. Paint the box in bright colours, and decorate it with tissue paper, beads, ribbons and sequins. Then think of a scene that could be performed from your pageant cart. You could even make some tiny cardboard people to act it out!

# Carnival!

Fancy-dress parades, decorated floats, steel bands, singers and masked dancers fill the street. Carnival has come to town! In many ways, modern carnivals are very like the European pageants of long ago. Gaily decorated carts, called floats, similar to the one pictured below, form a long procession. Each float carries costumed performers who entertain the watching crowds as the float passes by. Everyone joins in the singing and dancing, making carnival a colourful, noisy celebration. As well as singing and dancing, the performers often put on short plays, or sketches.

Annual carnivals are held in many towns and cities all over the world. Some carnivals, like the ones held in Trinidad and Rio de Janeiro, Brazil, are very famous. Trinidad's carnival starts at dawn on a Monday and lasts for two days and nights. By the end, everyone is completely exhausted!

This float is part of a carnival procession in Malta

## Mardi Gras

Another famous carnival is held in New Orleans in the United States of America. It is called Mardi Gras, which means fat Tuesday. It takes place on the Tuesday before the start of the Christian season of Lent, when Christians traditionally fast and pray. The original idea behind the Mardi Gras celebration was that everyone should have a good time before Lent began. As in Trinidad, decorated floats like this one tour the streets. Some carry musicians playing lively music called jazz. People dress up in extravagant costumes made from brightly-coloured fabric decorated with sequins and feathers. Everyone spends weeks before Mardi Gras getting their costumes ready.

A Mardi Gras float in New Orleans, USA

## What big heads!

These people are wearing huge head-masks made from a hardened mixture of paper and glue called papier mâché. They are worn at a festival called the Ten Day Celebrations which takes place once a year in Taiwan. In Spain, carnival performers wear similar heads representing King Ferdinand and Queen Isabella, who ruled Spain in the 1400s. Other head-masks represent the Moors, who occupied parts of Spain until King Ferdinand drove them out in 1492. Sometimes the two groups in this carnival procession perform a mock battle. The heads are so heavy that the performers have difficulty keeping their balance.

Performers celebrating the Ten Day Celebrations in Taiwan

# Living history

Imagine you are standing high on a hillside looking down on the busy scene shown here. The noise of wooden poles crashing together fills the air, while men shout out as they charge into battle. The fighting certainly looks dangerous! But this is one battle in which no one will get hurt, because these people are acting. They are taking part in a historical reconstruction of a real battle. Their stage is the site where the original battle actually took place.

## Bringing history alive

The picture below shows another historical reconstruction. The actors, or cast, in both these scenes make sure that the clothes they wear and the weapons they carry are as close as possible to the real thing used hundreds of years ago.

They are bringing history alive for people to see, hear and touch. To do this they must study the history of the event very carefully so that they can re-enact exactly what happened. They rehearse everything down to the smallest detail – especially if they are staging a battle, because they must make sure that no one gets hurt even if they look as though they are fighting fiercely.

Performers at the Guadalupe festival in Mexico City

Members of the English Civil War Society re-enacting a battle

This man is using a printing press in a museum in Shropshire, England

## Plays in a museum

In many museums you will find actors helping to bring the exhibits to life. This man, for example, is showing how a printing press was used in the 1800s. Printing machines like this, in which the letters are all set by hand, are not widely used today. But by the time the visitors leave the museum, they will appreciate what a slow and skilled job printing used to be. Of course, the man is not printing to earn his living. He's an actor, and this corner of the museum is his stage. 'Living' history is exciting. Watch for chances to see it and, perhaps, even join in.

# The circus

Have you been to the circus and watched all the different acts that are performed in the arena? A circus ring is full of colour, action and noise. Laugh at the tumbling clowns with their slapstick comedy. Hold your breath as the acrobats and bareback riders do impossible balancing acts.

Circus acrobats perform for a theatre audience

## The history of the circus

Although acrobats and jugglers performed in Ancient Greece, and in China some 2,000 years ago, it was a long time before somebody had the idea of bringing the separate acts together and presenting them as a theatrical spectacle. This happened in the late 1700s when many European theatres were built with huge circus rings in front of the stage. Here acrobats perform daring feats right above the heads of a theatre audience.

## From town to town

Circuses did not stay inside theatre buildings for long. In time, the number of acts expanded to include trained animals, and these needed special cages and equipment. So most circuses moved out into the open and performed inside huge tents called big tops. In Europe in the 1800s, more and more railway lines were being laid, and the circuses found it easier to travel around and take the show to the audience. Special circus trains were built to carry the heavy equipment from one town to the next. The largest circuses needed as many as 100 railway wagons!

Acrobats in a Chinese circus

On reaching a new town, the circus would parade from the station to the field. Everyone would turn out to watch the elephants pass by, then the horses, the clowns, the jugglers and the cages of wild animals. No one could miss the fact that the circus was in town!

Once on the site, the roustabouts took over. Roustabouts were the crew of skilled tent builders who struggled to put up the huge, gaily coloured big top. They also had to put together the huge ring that formed the stage, and the tiers of seating for the audience around this ring. Finally, they put up the canvas-walled corridor, known as the connection by circus people. The performers would enter the big top through this as each act began.

## The circus today

The great days of the travelling circus are over. The last of the big travelling shows in America, Ringling's, stopped touring in 1956, and England's largest circus, Bertram Mills, stopped in 1964.

However, there are many smaller circuses still travelling around in trucks and caravans. Today, many people dislike seeing trained animals performing tricks, so their place has been taken by human performers – trapeze artists, trick cyclists and daredevil acts such as juggling with knives and fire-eating. The photograph above shows acrobats in a modern Chinese circus. Of course, the most popular of all the circus performers are still the clowns.

# Clowns

Do you recognize the characters in this picture? Do they make you laugh? They should, for these are clowns – probably the funniest actors of all. Nothing ever goes right for the clowns. These three are pretending to stick up posters, but the glue is splashing everywhere and the ladder is toppling over. What a disaster!

Some of the first clowns we know about appeared in the processions that took place before plays in Ancient Greece. In Ancient Rome, clowns appeared in some plays as comic servants called fools. By the 1600s, the fool was usually dressed in strange, colourful clothes, and carried a rattle made from a pig's bladder so that the audience could recognize him straight away.

These early clowns were just jokers telling funny stories. Later, clowns began to spice up their stories with exaggerated actions to add to the fun. Clowns don't often appear in the theatre any more. You are more likely to see them at the circus, or performing on street corners or at festivals.

These Spanish clowns are pretending to stick up posters

A French clown

## Different clowns

Nowadays, there are all sorts of different clowns. Most use thick make-up called greasepaint to change their appearance for a show. Their make-up is colourful so that it can be seen from far away, and each clown develops an individual clown face. Some paint their faces white and mark their eyes, mouth and cheeks with brilliant red greasepaint. They wear vividly-coloured costumes and are known as whiteface clowns. They are the ones who are always trying to be helpful, but who just end up getting in the way.

You may have seen clowns wearing baggy costumes and oversized shoes. Imagine trying to walk or even run in a pair of shoes which are three or four sizes too big. They are the August clowns, named after a famous French clown called Auguste who performed in the 1800s.

## Paint a clown face

Design your own individual clown face. You will need to cut a face shape from a stiff piece of card. First, cut holes for your eyes and mouth. Now sketch a few ideas for your clown's make-up. When you are happy with your design, use crayons to colour in the face. Choose bold, bright colours. Attach the card to a stick, and you have a permanent clown face that you can use whenever you feel like playing the fool!

# Famous clowns

Joseph Grimaldi

Imagine playing a game of leap-frog with a giant frog! Now that would really make you laugh! The clown pictured below is doing just this. The illustration shows a clown called Joseph Grimaldi performing in a Christmas pantomime called *Harlequin and the Golden Fish.* This performance took place in 1811. Of course, the frog wasn't real – it was an actor in costume. In later shows, the frog began to appear dressed in a hat, which made the audiences laugh even more.

Joseph Grimaldi was one of the most famous of all clowns. He was born in England in 1778 and first appeared on stage when he was four years old. Part of his act was to build an object using all kinds of odds and ends he had collected on stage, puffing and panting as he worked. A favourite piece of fun was to make a cart from a basket, using four round cheeses as the wheels, and then try to ride in it. You might know Grimaldi by his other name – Joey the Clown.

Joseph Grimaldi in *Harlequin and the Golden Fish*

## Arlecchino

This colourful character is called Arlecchino, or Harlequin. Arlecchino was made famous by bands of commedia dell'arte actors who began to tour Italy in the 1500s. Clowns helped commedia dell'arte become popular in countries around Italy. Since they used actions rather than words, it did not matter if the audiences spoke a different language. Comedy is a language all of its own!

Arlecchino, a character from commedia dell'arte

# Pantomime

"Oh yes, it is!" hisses the stage villain. "Oh no, it isn't!" yell the audience. The villain tries again, this time snarling even louder. The audience of children roar their reply. They know the villain won't get away with his evil tricks, and that the hero will win in the end, and their excited response is part of the show. It's fun to feel they are contributing to what is happening on stage!

This is pantomime, a colourful show which fills British theatres once a year at Christmas time. Pantomime is a particular kind of show which is seen nowhere else in the world. It is a mixture of songs, dances, knockabout comedy and circus acts, all woven around well-known children's stories. Among the most popular pantomimes are *Aladdin*, *Cinderella* and *Jack and the Beanstalk*. This picture shows a performance of *Cinderella*.

'Pantomime' was painted by Judy Joel

## The origins of pantomime

Pantomime developed out of the clown performances in Italian commedia dell'arte. The first pantomimes, then called harlequinades, were performed in England in the early 1700s. The main characters at this time were Harlequin and Columbine. Turn to page 34 to read more about commedia dell'arte.

Pantomime actors have always worn extravagant costumes – some even dress as animals. You can see a cow and two mice in the performance of *Cinderella*. Sometimes real animals are brought onto the stage!

Scenery and stage props are always elaborate and colourful. Special effects called transformation scenes are a feature of pantomime. In *Cinderella*, for example, the scene changes from Cinderella's kitchen to the Prince's ballroom as if by magic. This is done with clever lighting and with special hinged scenery which is easy to move.

## Figures of fun

You'll find that similar characters crop up in different pantomimes. There is a comic female figure, called the Dame, who is always acted by a man. She is a bossy, exaggerated character who talks very loudly and wears amazing clothes. In *Cinderella*, there are two dames – Cinderella's two ugly sisters. They constantly order Cinderella around. The principal boy character – this is Prince Charming in *Cinderella* – is played by a woman. Extra characters are often included in the pantomime just to make an excuse for more clowning and fun.

## The audience

Children are the most important people in a pantomime audience. But the actors want to entertain everyone, so they usually tell jokes about well-known people and events in the news which will appeal to the adults too. Actors like playing in pantomime, because they know that it brings many people to the theatre who might not usually go. For children, a pantomime is often a first introduction to drama, so actors take special care to make sure they have a good time.

# The art of puppetry

Have you ever seen a puppet show? If you have, you have watched one of the oldest forms of theatre in the world. Instead of actors, the story is told by hand-made toys called puppets. There are many different types of puppets, ranging from those which are as small as your finger to ones which are almost life-size. They are made from all sorts of materials, including fabric, leather and wood, and are made to move by skilled operators called puppeteers. They usually appear on special stages to a background of words and music.

A marionette puppeteer with his puppet

A group of marionettes

## Marionettes

The picture on the left shows a group of puppets called marionettes. Marionettes are probably the oldest kind of puppets known today. They were used over 2,000 years ago in Ancient Egypt, in Ancient Greece, and by the Hindus in India, although these early marionettes were probably operated with just one string. In Europe, marionettes became very popular after the 1600s. Marionette shows are very exciting, so if you have a chance to see one, make sure you go along.

Marionettes are usually carved out of wood, but some are made of a hardened mixture of paper and glue called papier mâché. You can see that the heads, legs and arms are flexible and are attached to strings. Look at the way the arms bend at the elbows and wrists, just like human arms.

The strings lead upwards to a stick called a crutch. You cannot see the puppeteers because they are hidden. Each puppeteer controls one puppet, making it move by holding the crutch with one hand and plucking at the strings with the other. You can see how this works in the picture on the left. Do you think it looks an easy skill to learn? It's not! Most marionettes have nine strings, and some have more. Learning to move these strings so that the puppet moves smoothly takes a lot of patience and practice.

A street entertainer with jigging puppets

## Jigging puppets

If you had walked down a city street in Europe in the 1700s and 1800s, you might well have seen a performer with a row of jigging puppets. These puppets were small figures with flexible limbs, just like the ones shown above. They were attached to a string which was held between a short post and the performer's knee. When the performer played a tune, he jerked his knee to pull the string and make the puppets dance.

### Make a row of jigging puppets

Think of two or three characters who will make up your own row of jigging puppets. Draw the body and head of each figure on a piece of card.

Your figures will need to be about 25 centimetres tall. Draw the arms and legs separately and then paint on features and clothes. You could glue sequins and ribbons onto the costumes to make them look more special. Cut out the pieces and loosely attach the arms and legs to the body with paper fasteners.

Now make two holes in the shoulders of each figure, and thread a long piece of string through these holes. Attach one end to a post, and the other to your knee. You are ready to make your jigging puppets dance.

# Glove puppets

Punch

These children are watching a Punch and Judy show

Pull a sock onto your hand, stick on two buttons to form eyes, and you have made the simplest puppet of all – a glove puppet! The puppets pictured here are called glove puppets, but they have hollow papier mâché heads and bodies made from fabric. The puppeteer moves the puppet with one finger fitting inside the head and a finger and thumb inside the hands. Sometimes the puppets have legs. On a tiny stage, with the puppeteer hidden below, the puppets look as if they are moving on their own.

The story behind a Punch and Judy show is very simple, because the puppeteer can only make two puppets move at the same time. One hand makes Punch move. The other operates puppets representing all the other characters. Traditionally, these are Punch's wife, Judy, their baby, a policeman, and a crocodile. If you see a Punch and Judy show, you will be encouraged to join in and shout back at the puppets. Shout loudly – your replies are an important part of the act.

Judy

## Punch and Judy

The children sitting in front of the small booth are enjoying a glove puppet theatre show called Punch and Judy. Punch and Judy has been a popular street show in England since the late 1600s when travelling puppeteers began to take the show to fairs and festivals. Punch, a rough, quarrelsome character with a hooked nose and a hump, probably developed from Pulcinella, a character in Italian commedia dell'arte. He is well known in other countries, too. The French call him Guignol, and in Germany his name is Kasperl while the Russians call him Petrushka.

# Bunraku puppets

This picture show a performance of bunraku

Two large, gaily-dressed puppets are brought onto the stage, and begin to move in a series of complicated gestures. A team of people called chanters starts to recite the lines of a play, and a musician picks out a melody on a three-stringed instrument called a samisen. A performance of bunraku has begun!

Bunraku puppets can be found in the theatres of Osaka in Japan. These amazing puppets stand well over one metre tall and can make so many different movements that three people are needed to operate each puppet. It's not hard to guess that one of the first skills that these puppeteers have to learn is how to keep out of each other's way!

## Bunraku puppeteers

As you can see in the picture of a bunraku performance, the chief puppeteers wear black costumes. Each has two assistants dressed in black and wear hoods to hide their faces. It takes three puppeteers to operate one puppet since each is responsible for different parts of the puppet's body. Between them, they can make the puppets roll their eyes and open their mouths, changing their expressions completely. The puppets can also be made to carry out all the movements that a human body can do! It is fascinating to watch, and the audience quickly learns to ignore the puppeteers.

## The history of bunraku

Puppet plays telling stories of the battles of Japanese history have been performed for over 300 years. At first, the puppets were controlled from above with strings, rather like marionettes, and the puppeteers were hidden. But in time the puppet-makers started to make their puppets more life-like. By about 1750 the marionettes had become too complicated to work with strings, so the only answer was for the operators to appear with them on stage. You can see the rods used to control a bunraku puppet in this picture.

## A long performance

If you are lucky enough to see a bunraku performance in Japan, be prepared to sit still for a long time. Each show can last up to twelve hours! They require a lot of preparation, and several teams of puppeteers and chanters take part. Bunraku was almost unknown outside Japan until the 1960s, when a group of bunraku players took their show to Europe. They had to prepare a specially shortened programme, cutting the usual twelve hours to three hours to suit European audiences. The shows were a great success.

A bunraku puppet

# Shadows on the stage

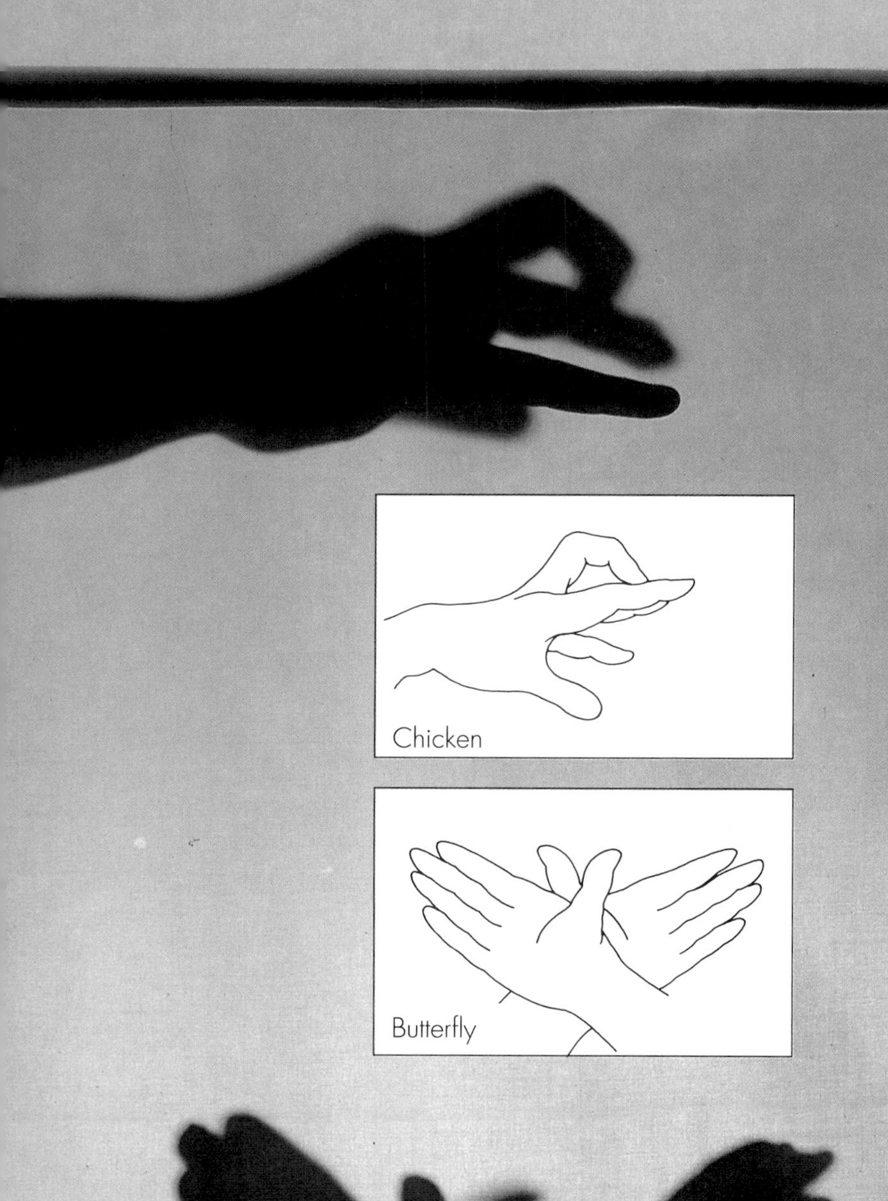


You have probably played the game of moving your hands to make animal-head shadows on a wall. With practice, you can make the heads appear to move very realistically. Use our suggestions to form a chicken's head and a butterfly.

Take this a step further by placing a screen of white cotton in front of a torch. If you sit behind the screen, but in front of the torch, you will be able to make shadows on the screen with your hands. Your audience can watch from the opposite side of the screen, so that all they see are the shadows. Remember to keep your head out of the way!

## Flat puppets

What you have created is known as a shadow show. Performances of this kind are amongst the oldest forms of theatre we know of. In the ancient world they were performed in China, India, Turkey and Egypt. They are still popular today in Indonesia, where they are called wayang. They are performed by puppeteers who use flat leather or parchment puppets to throw shadows onto screens. You can see an Indonesian puppeteer holding two shadow puppets in the picture on the opposite page. The inset shows you what the audience sees. These flat puppets move their limbs when the puppeteer pulls on the rods. They are a form of marionette and are usually about half a metre tall.

This Malaysian puppeteer is operating two shadow puppets

Inset: A Malaysian shadow-puppet play

## Setting up a shadow show

The screen required for a shadow show is simple, so it can easily be set up wherever the puppeteer has been invited to perform. First a thin white cloth, about the size of a single bed sheet, is stretched over a wooden frame. The bottom of the screen is placed about shoulder height. The space below is filled in so that the puppeteer remains hidden. An oil lamp is hung behind the screen to cast the shadows, and the audience take their seats on the other side. Oil lamps have been used in shadow shows for many hundreds of years. It's easy to see why. They throw a strong, warm glow onto the screen and this is perfect for making shadows.

Apart from a small band which provides the music, shadow shows only need one person – the puppeteer. In Indonesia this person is known as the dalang. The dalang sings and chants the story while operating the puppets, and even manages to tap a small hammer to keep the musicians in time. The shadow puppets are introduced one by one, and each performs a dance. Then the story begins. This is usually based on a religious story, but most dalangs make up the words as they go along. Would you like to try performing with shadow puppets? You will need a lot of energy. Wayangs begin at sunset and can last for anything up to ten hours!

A Turkish shadow puppet

# Toy theatres

This engraving shows a toy theatre performance of *The Miller and his Men*

Just think how exciting it would be to stage a play in your own home. You would be in control of all the characters' movements. The words, sound, scenery and lighting would all be your responsibility, too. It would be quite a job! Perhaps it would be easier to take charge of a miniature theatre like the one in the picture above. It is known as toy theatre or juvenile drama.

This souvenir sheet was printed with characters taken from *Oliver Twist* by Charles Dickens

## How toy theatres began

If you had watched a play in London, England, in the late 1700s, you would have received a souvenir sheet showing the principal character in the play. When you got home, you might have stuck the figure onto card, cut it out and decorated it with fabric and metallic paper to produce what was known as a tinsel portrait. Toy theatres probably developed from this idea. Like the souvenir sheets, they were printed on cardboard and could be cut out and assembled at home.

## Theatre in miniature

A hundred years later, toy theatres became a popular form of theatrical entertainment throughout Europe and the United States of America. You can see a fully-assembled toy theatre below. This particular theatre was designed in 1860 and shows a performance of a well-known fairytale, *Sleeping Beauty.*

Toy theatres were often miniature versions of real stage productions of the time. The characters in the play were printed on flat card, and could be cut out at home. The characters were attached to lengths of wire, so that they could be pushed onto the stage from the side of the theatre, or the wings.

A toy theatre dating from 1860, set up for a performance of *Sleeping Beauty*

## Presenting toy theatre

It only took one person to put on a toy theatre performance, but it was easier with two people, one standing either side of the theatre. They were often screened from the audience by a curtain – as you can see in the picture opposite. As in a real play, the words, or lines, had to be rehearsed before the first performance. When everything was ready, the curtain was pulled up and the show began. Each time one of the figures 'spoke', it had to be moved up and down so that the audience could easily tell which character was meant to be speaking!

## Build your own toy theatre

It's very easy to make a toy theatre at home, and it can be used again and again. First of all, you need to choose a favourite story to present in your toy theatre. Then cut out oblong sections from the front and sides of a large cardboard box. Paint an arch over the hole in the front, and paint the inside of the box. You might like to choose different colours for the walls and for the floor. You could also place it on another box to form a raised stage. We made four footlights from semi-circles of card covered with silver foil.

Now find three pieces of card the size of the box, and use sticky tape to attach these to rods or sticks. These rods rest on grooves cut in the top of the box. Paint a scene on one of the cards to form a backdrop. Cut and paint two more to form wings – you can see a wing in front of the theatre here. Next, draw your characters on cardboard, paint them, and cut them out. Attach each one to a rod. You can push the figures on stage from the holes in the side of the box. Finally attach two pieces of fabric to another rod to form a curtain. Now enjoy staging your very own play.

# CHAPTER FOUR

# THE ACTOR'S CRAFT

There's a lot of skill in acting. It may look as if the performers just walk on stage, deliver their lines, and walk off again. But think of all the hard work that goes on behind the scenes. Actors have to learn to move properly and how to project the voice so that all the audience can hear.

Different styles of acting call for different skills. Some plays are acted in a 'realistic' way, while others require actors to stick to a more formal or traditional style. Find out how props and costumes help to create an image, and how masks and make-up add the final touches to an actor's performance.

# The art of acting

The English actor Leo McKern

The actor finishes the final act with a dramatic flourish. The audience are captivated and clap loudly to show their appreciation. The whole cast was magnificent!

Do you ever stop to wonder what makes a good actor or actress? Of course, actors have to have natural talent, but they also need to learn special techniques to help improve their performances. Remember, actors are ordinary people. They have families and friends and homes, just like you. But when they are acting on stage, they have to pretend to be other people, perhaps with very different kinds of lives from their own.

It's not always easy to do this. For example, an actress might be going through a sad time in her own life, but she must play a happy role each night at the theatre. That can be difficult. Actors have to try hard to persuade you, in the audience, that they really are who they're pretending to be. If they just stood on the stage and spoke their lines, they might not convince anyone! So they use special methods, collectively known as the art of acting, to help them play a part, or role, more successfully.

## Playing a role

While make-up, costume and props can all help to make roles more convincing, these things are not always necessary.

An actor must also learn basic acting skills in order to portray a character properly. One of the most important skills to learn is the correct way to move. Actors must think about the way they walk, sit down, even how they stand still. They must think about the expressions on their faces and the gestures they make with their hands. What do the poses of these actors show you? Leo McKern looks as if he is relating some exciting adventure. The woman in the picture below is full of love, or perhaps it's pity, and the man looks very guilty. Their poses tell us as much as their expressions. But perhaps most important of all is an actor's voice. You can learn more about this on pages 120 to 121.

These actors are using gestures to help their roles

This Japanese actor is preparing for a performance

## The audience's response

An actor's performance is seldom the same twice running, but often this has more to do with the audience than with the actor. Different audiences can change the way an actor plays a part. Actors often talk about 'good' audiences who react to what is happening on stage. They laugh when the play is funny. They sympathize with characters who are unhappy. They pay attention to the story. When good actors play to a good audience, everyone in the theatre feels they are sharing the same successful experience. Remember this the next time you see a play.

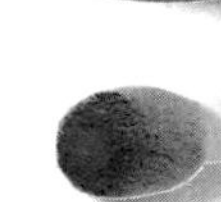

# The first actors

Voice, make-up, movement, facial expression – actors today are trained to use all of these and other methods to create a role in a play. But have actors always relied on training? Did the very first actors use these same skills?

No one knows who the very first actors were. Way back in time, people told stories and acted them out. We know from paintings that have been found in caves, that prehistoric people sometimes dressed up as animals and acted out hunting scenes to bring good luck at the actual hunt. Aboriginal people in Australia still perform dance-dramas like this today. They paint their bodies, and decorate themselves with feathers and plants. Sometimes the actors pretend to be animals as a way of honouring that animal's spirit. Or they might perform a short comic drama about an everyday event. Knowledge of the dances is passed down by word of mouth from the older members of the tribe to the children.

These Aborigines are performing a dance-drama based on old legends

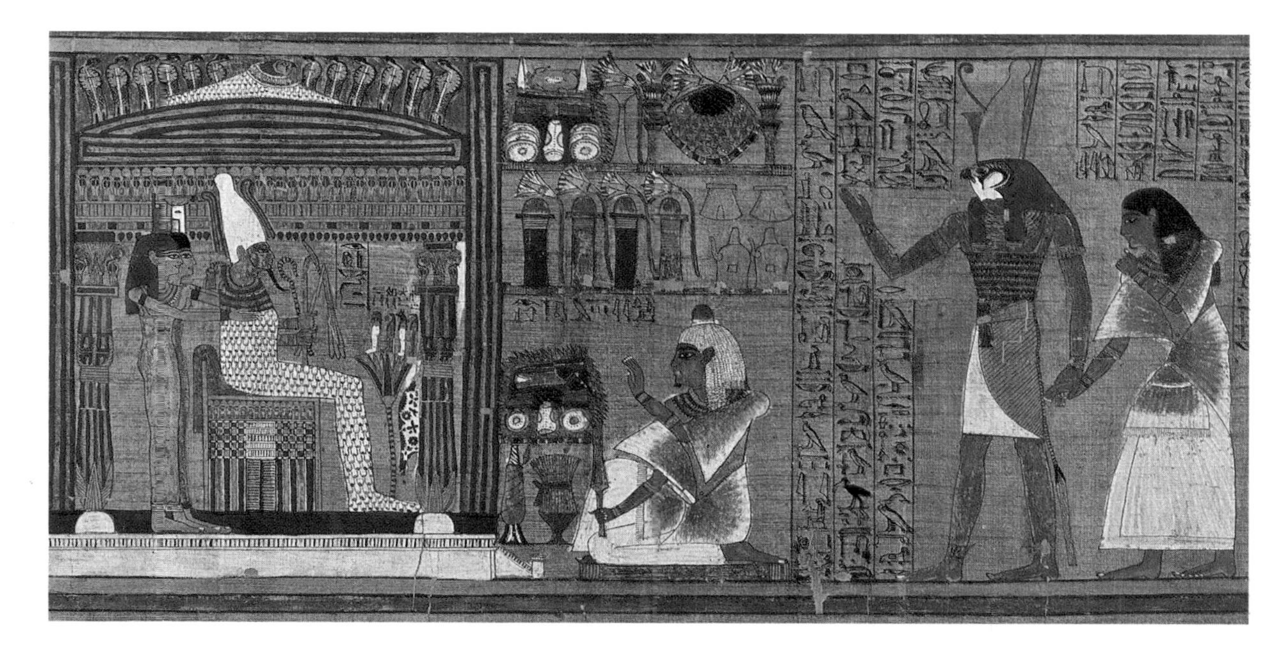

This Ancient Egyptian scroll shows the god Osiris seated on his throne

## Ritual drama

Long ago, in Ancient Egypt, actors were asked to perform rituals to honour their gods. Archaeologists have found the texts of some of these rituals preserved among the buried relics of the pyramids. One of them, the Abydos Passion Play, told of the god Osiris. Osiris was killed by his wicked brother Seth, but his wife Isis and his son Horus managed to bring him back to life again. You can see Osiris seated on his throne in the picture above. Like the Aboriginal dance-dramas, the Egyptian plays were intended to explain life and religion. They certainly weren't staged as pure entertainment!

## Ancient Greek plays

The first real actors we know about lived in Ancient Greece about 2,500 years ago. They acted in plays which included words, music, song and dance. The earliest stories were taken from Greek myths and legends, such as the story of the travels of King Odysseus. Later, the plays were about life in Ancient Greece at that time.

The female figure you can see in this picture is actually a man. Actors in Ancient Greece were always men. They wore elaborate costumes and masks which they would change as they switched roles. Plays were performed in huge, open-air theatres. To train their voices, actors would go up into the hills or down by the seashore. Here they would practise throwing their voices so that they could be heard over a long distance.

## Early drama in China

Historians tell us that drama was popular in Ancient China, too. The first performances grew out of ceremonies to worship the Chinese gods. They included music, dancing, juggling and acrobatic acts, sometimes with short plays acted in between. Later, the plays themselves became more important than the dancing and acrobatics. These were performed by trained actors who wore special make-up which identified the characters they were playing.

A Greek actor

# Voice projection

This Peking Opera performer has to project her voice to the listening audience

Imagine that you are watching an exciting play. The main character has a strong, clear voice which carries clearly around the theatre. It is full of expression and marvellous to listen to. But a second actor on the stage mumbles his lines and you can only pick out two words in every three. You become more and more annoyed as you start to lose the thread of the story.

Things like this can completely spoil one's enjoyment and understanding of a play – which is why actors have to make sure they can be heard in every part of a theatre. Their voices must carry. This does not mean merely speaking more loudly or shouting. It means speaking in an entirely different way from normal. It involves an acting skill called voice projection – a skill which most actors have to learn.

## Projecting your voice

When you have a conversation with a friend, there is no need for you to throw your voice very far. You might not want anyone else to hear what you are saying, so you keep your voice low, using only a small amount of breath. Actors have to project their voices over far greater distances whether they are speaking loudly or softly. To do this, they learn to breathe deeply using a muscle below their lungs called the diaphragm. You can feel this muscle if you put your hand just below your chest. If you fill your lungs with air and sing a loud note, you will feel your diaphragm vibrating.

These actors are rehearsing in Uganda

## Speaking clearly

Try saying 'bin'. Now say 'paw'. Think about the different way you shape your mouth when you say these two sounds. Now try again, this time holding a feather or a small mirror just in front of your mouth. When you say 'bin', you'll probably find that nothing will happen. But when you say 'paw', the feather will move and the mirror will mist up. This is because a lot more air is coming out of your mouth.

## Breath control

Now try some breath control. Ask an adult if you can light a candle. Take a deep breath and breathe across the candle flame so that it bends. You'll have to let your breath out very evenly and gently. If you blow too hard, the flame will go out. Try varying how quickly you let out your breath and watch how it affects the flame.

Many people are lazy when they speak. They don't take the trouble to use the tongue, teeth and lips to form sounds properly. Lazy speech is no good in the theatre, and actors have to learn to pronounce their words clearly. They do this by practising different sounds aloud, and by using techniques like those with the candle to help them think about the ways in which sounds are formed.

## Facing the audience

The group of actors above are learning another skill. They are facing outwards from the stage and playing to the audience. Actors have to do this whenever they want to say something or carry out a particular action which the audience should not miss. It is not an easy skill to pick up – at first it feels strange to face a big audience in a theatre building. But after three or four performances, it begins to feel a natural part of the pretend stage world.

# Body movement

Pretend for a moment that you are very old and weak. Your bones creak and your muscles ache. Now try to walk in character. You will have to hobble along slowly, perhaps pausing to rest. If you skip casually along, no one will believe that you're acting the part of an old person. It is easy to see why the way in which actors move is so important.

Movement and gesture are particularly important in certain traditional plays. This is especially true of Indian dance-dramas called Kathakali and Kathak, both of which are shown here. The performers in these dance-dramas use the same complicated gestures as Indian actors have used for hundreds of years. Learning to do this is not an easy task for young performers new to the stage.

These students are learning movements for an Indian dance-drama called Kathak

## Training to be a Kathakali actor

Singers, actors and musicians are all involved in a performance of Kathakali. Two singers sing and speak the words of the play, while male actors mime and dance, fitting their movements exactly to the voices of the singers. These actors start training when they are about 12 years old. It takes them six years or more to learn some 600 different hand gestures and eye movements! They also have to follow a fitness programme to keep their bodies supple, and to build up their stamina for the long performances. A Kathakali performance can last all night. Even the training sessions start before dawn and often go on until midnight!

## The first performance

When their teacher decides that they are good enough to perform in public, the students are allowed to take part in the dances that start every Kathakali show. From then on, they slowly build up their careers until they are experienced enough to take important parts in the plays, such as those of the warriors, demons or wise men. Then they join a group of travelling actors to perform in temples, halls or rich private homes.

This picture shows an experienced Kathakali performer

# Facial expression

When you talk to another person, you usually look into their eyes, and try to read their expression. You know when someone is angry by the tone of their voice, but you also pick up clues from the expression on their face. In the same way, actors use facial expressions to help the audience understand the character they are portraying.

## Happy or sad?

Look at the scene below taken from a Japanese play. What do you think is going on? The two actors at the front of the stage are in trouble. They have been caught thieving and are firmly tied up. But look at the expressions on their faces. They are both roaring with laughter. Far from being alarmed by their situation, they appear to be highly amused!

The scene is taken from a comic play, called a Kyogen, and it shows how important an actor's facial expressions are. You would read the scene very differently if you could see fear on the faces of the thieves.

A scene from a Japanese Kyogen play

The expression on the face of these characters shows clearly what each one is feeling.

**1.** Sadness
**2.** Hatred
**3.** Admiration
**4.** Interest
**5.** Scorn

## Learning to show emotion

What emotions do you think are expressed on the faces above? The answers are given in the numbered captions. Do you think they look true-to-life? In the past actors used to study drawings similar to these to try and memorize the expressions they should show on stage.

## Practise facial expression

Nowadays, many actors practise changing their expression in front of a mirror. This helps them to exercise their facial muscles as well. You could try doing this with a friend. Sit in front of a mirror and ask your friend to call out each of the emotions shown above. Try forming these on your face, switching quickly from one expression to another. You'll find that it's not easy to do this on demand, but it's the kind of thing an actor often has to do.

# Using masks

This masked dancer is taking part in a festival in Bhutan

On the previous page, you read about the ways in which actors change their facial expressions to show different emotions. Sometimes actors achieve the same result wearing a mask. This hides the face but still manages to tell the audience who the character is or what the character is feeling. Have you ever worn a mask? It is a strange feeling. You are just the same person behind it, but when people look at you they see someone different.

## Traditional masked drama

The incredible mask in the picture above is worn each year at a religious fair called the Paro Tsechu festival, held in the country of Bhutan. At this festival, masked dancers enact a play which tells the story of a wicked hunter. This hunter changes his behaviour and learns to respect animals instead of killing them after a meeting with a wise old man. The story is based on the Buddhist belief that all living things are sacred.

A selection of Ancient Greek masks

## Why wear a mask?

People have been making and wearing masks for many thousands of years. They were originally worn to perform religious dances. Later, these dances were staged for entertainment rather than for worship. Hidden behind their masks, performers found it easier to enter into the mood of the dance. And the masks added extra excitement for the audience, making the dancers look larger than life.

The masks pictured above are drawings of masks which were used about 2,000 years ago in Ancient Greece. Look at the way the features are exaggerated. Greek and Roman audiences would recognize each mask immediately and know exactly what kind of character – wise or foolish, honest or cunning – they were watching.

## Make a mask

It's fun making and decorating masks to use for your own drama performances. The easiest kind to make is one cut from a sheet of thick paper or thin card, with holes for the eyes, nose and mouth. Our mask is based on the drawings of the Greek masks. The string hair is attached with strong glue. Remember to punch a hole at each side and thread elastic through to hold the mask against your face.

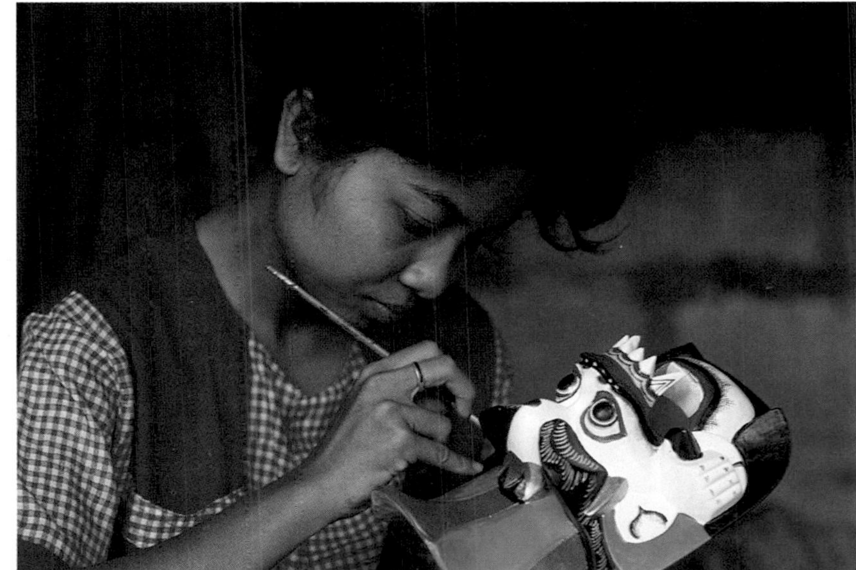

This woman is painting a mask in Bali, Indonesia

# Painting the face

A collection of Chinese make-up masks

Take a look at these colourful miniature masks. Each one is the size of a ping-pong ball, and is beautifully painted. Chinese actors sometimes refer to masks similar to these when they make up their own faces. Each style of painted mask has a particular meaning, and the actor needs to copy the right mask reference for the character to be played.

## Why make-up is important

Actors have been painting their faces for thousands of years. In the 1600s, French comedy actors even used flour to whiten their faces! Make-up helps the audience to identify the various characters in a play, and to see the actors' features. In many theatres, the audience sits at some distance from the stage. The actors' faces can become indistinct and rather pale under the strong artificial lights which flood the stage, although some theatres today have lighting systems which do not do this.

Make-up also disguises an actor's true features, making a young person look old, or a healthy person look sick. Make-up can even be symbolic, with the colours and final design chosen having a special meaning, as shown by the Chinese painted masks.

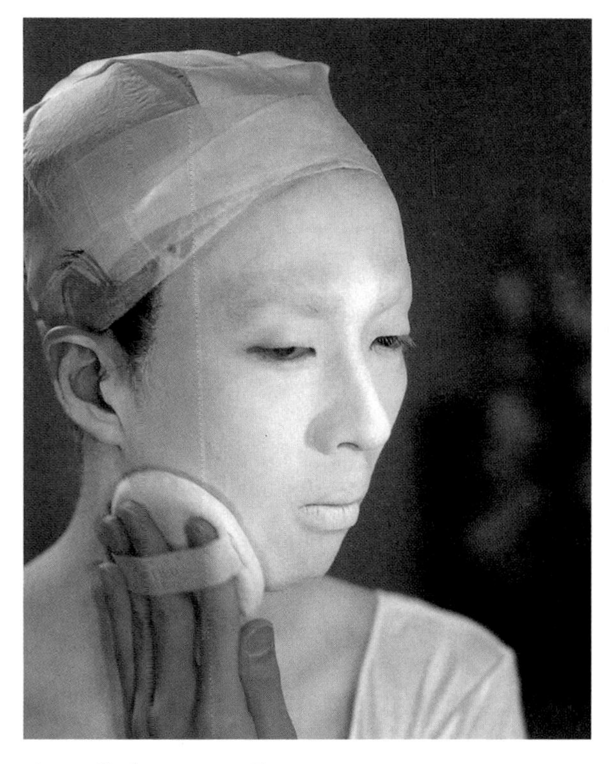

This Kabuki actor is putting on his stage make-up

## Applying make-up

Most actors apply their own make-up, using a special form of make-up called greasepaint which comes in sticks or palettes. You can see some examples of different types of greasepaint in the pictures below. Putting on make-up can take a long time, but it helps an actor to get into the character and it is an important part of an actor's craft.

The pictures above show two stages of a Japanese Kabuki actor putting on his make-up. He has covered his hair in order to pull it back from the face, and in the first picture he is coating his face with a thick white greasepaint. He has even covered his lips and eyebrows! In the second picture, the actor is carefully painting in his features – bright red lips and jet black eyebrows. When he is performing on stage, these features will show up clearly to the audience.

## A real shiner!

Why don't you try using make-up to give yourself a spectacular black eye? You can either sit in front of a mirror to do this, or try it on a friend. You will need cream make-up in black, purple, yellow and brown. Make sure it is a kind which can be washed off afterwards with soap and water. First, pat black and purple colours onto the skin around the eye with your fingertips, taking care not to get any in the eye. Blend the edges of the colours into each other, but be careful not to lose the individual colours completely. Then add yellow and brown to highlight the bruise. You'll be surprised how real it looks.

# Properties

The English actor Leo McKern

Rolls of paper, a briefcase, a lighted taper – this actor has so much to carry that he is even holding some documents in his mouth! Do you think that he looks absorbed in the role he is playing? He's acting the part of a busy and important defence lawyer and is using a whole range of objects to help create a believable character.

Objects like these are called properties, or props. Most theatre companies keep a store of props which can be used in different performances. There are all sorts of props. You may have seen an actor wearing an unusual pair of glasses, or even using a walking stick, although you know that actor does not wear glasses or need a walking stick in real life. Together with costume and make-up, these props help an actor to slip into a role.

## Can you spot a fake?

Do you think the carved picture frame pictured below is made from wood? It's actually made from plaster! The candle flame is lit by a battery. Sometimes the props you see are real, but when this is not possible, there are usually ways to fake them. Many plays are staged very cheaply and the actors can't afford to buy everything they need for each performance. They have to be ingenious and think of ways to fake their props.

It is usually possible to make authentic-looking props from cheap materials. If you act in a school play and you need a

dagger, you can make one from strong card, coated with silver paint. Papier mâché shaped over chicken wire is a simple way to make a realistic shield.

## Let's eat

Do you think that this plate of fish looks good enough to eat? You wouldn't find it very tasty. It is made of fabric and papier mâché! Stage food is usually faked. Do you know why? Imagine trying to act with the smell of rotten fish in your nostrils! Food goes bad very quickly under hot stage lights, and it is expensive to replace. It is much easier to have a plate of food which can be brought out again and again, and which only needs a quick dust!

This plate of fish is actually a stage prop

## Make a sea crown

Imagine you're playing Neptune, the Roman god of the sea. Here's a way to make his sea crown. First, use a tape measure to measure around your head. Add two centimetres to this and cut a narrow strip of flexible card to this length. Now draw fish shapes onto the card and carefully cut these shapes out. Paint your crown and decorate it with beads and sequins. Glue the ends together to form a loop and then hang more shapes from the crown with cotton thread. Add lengths of shiny ribbon to look like seaweed. We decorated our crown with pasta shells sprayed with gold and silver paint.

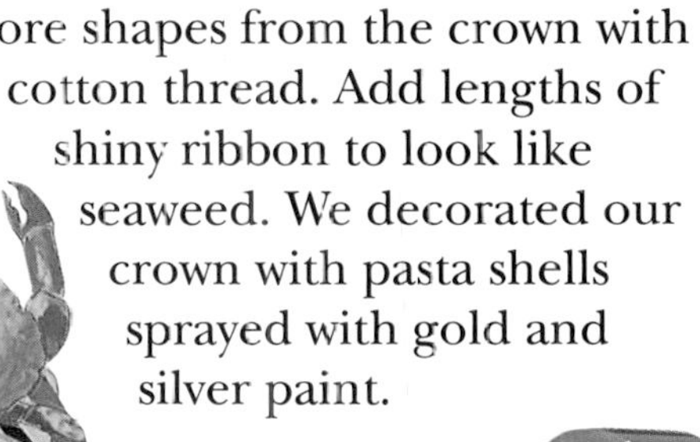

# Larger than life

*Dinorah* which was first performed in 1859

When you're in the theatre, you are watching a 'pretend' world. The performers' time on stage is limited. To hold your attention, a lot of action has to be crammed into a short time. A lot more happens on stage than normally happens in real life, and what takes place is usually far more interesting too. When this unreality is completely exaggerated, it is known as melodrama.

## Melodrama

You can see two scenes from different melodramas on these pages. Here a woman is about to hurtle into a waterfall in pursuit of her pet goat. Luckily, her true love arrives just in time to make a heroic rescue! The picture on the right shows a dramatic scene from a popular English melodrama called *Under the Gaslight.* How do you think the hero will escape? In fact, his girlfriend saves him just in time.

Melodramas are usually about 'baddies' such as outlaws and highwaymen, who are outwitted by brave, heroic 'goodies'. Often, one of the goodies has a friend who somehow gets trapped or captured, and is rescued at the last minute from a horrific fate. The plays are full of mystery and suspense, rather like the horror movies you might see today, with fights, chases, kidnappings, escapes and sad death scenes.

Players in melodrama exaggerate every gesture. They clasp their hands, fling out their arms and mop their brows. The villain will twirl his moustache and laugh menacingly. The young heroine is 'too good to be true'. When melodramas were first staged, the audience would hiss when the villain appeared and cheer for the hero and heroine. Music was used to exaggerate the important moments. Many melodramas were based on novels, so when they had seen the play, people could enjoy the story again by reading the book.

A scene from a melodrama called *Under the Gaslight*

## Spectacle

Writers of melodrama liked to compete with each other to introduce more and more spectacular scenes into their plays. The stories were set in front of huge sets of castle ruins, haunted houses or gloomy forests. Shipwrecks, earthquakes, fires, railway accidents and even horse-racing on stage were not unusual events. You can see an example of this on page 153. The ways of producing these special effects relied on different forms of lighting and complicated machinery.

The most exciting scenes from the play were reproduced on posters. These exaggerated these scenes even more, to tempt people to go to the theatre. One of these posters, which advertised a play called *Streets of London*, is pictured on the right. What melodramatic scenes can you see here?

## The end of melodrama

Melodrama was popular in Europe in the late 1800s but it disappeared almost as suddenly as it had begun. The reason was the invention of the cinema. Sensational scenes seemed even more dramatic on film than on the stage, and the early silent films were well-suited to melodramatic stories. Many old melodramas were made into films, using the same actors – and many of the theatres where melodramas were shown were turned into cinemas.

This theatre poster is advertising an English melodrama of the 1800s

# Styles of acting

The two photographs on these pages were taken in the early 1900s in Russia. The people are wearing clothes which were fashionable at that time. Can you imagine stepping into these rooms – perhaps sitting at the table in the picture on the right, or slipping into one of the more comfortable chairs in the picture below? The scenes certainly look very realistic.

In fact the two photographs are scenes from different plays which were directed by a Russian called Konstantin Stanislavsky. You can see a picture of Stanislavsky on the opposite page. Stanislavsky had many new and unusual ideas about acting. These appealed to the audiences of the 1880s who were beginning to lose interest in melodrama.

The Moscow Arts Theatre in a production of Chekhov's *The Three Sisters*, directed by Stanislavsky

## Plays of real life

The change from melodrama to real life began with writers like Henrik Ibsen, a Norwegian, and Gerhart Hauptmann from Germany. Both turned their back on imaginary worlds and started writing plays which were 'naturalistic' or 'realistic'. Their plays were usually set in the present day and not way back in history. Themes such as the problems of modern family life, were ones that the audience could understand and sympathize with. Of course these were not suited to the melodramatic style of acting. Actors in naturalistic plays were only convincing if they behaved like real people.

A scene from Anton Chekhov's play *The Cherry Orchard*, directed by Konstantin Stanislavsky

More than ever the actors had to study the characters they were playing and imagine themselves inside the characters' minds. If an actor was playing the part of a person who was mean with money, that actor needed to try to understand exactly what it was like to be so mean. If the character was badly depressed, the actor had to imagine what might have caused the depression and how it would affect one's behaviour.

## Stanislavsky

Konstantin Stanislavsky was one of the first drama teachers to train actors to think in this realistic way. He set up the Moscow Arts Theatre in 1898 to teach his ideas to actors. Stanislavsky wanted actors to try and become the character they were playing. If a character was sad, he encouraged the actor to think back to a personal experience of sadness. By remembering a time of real sadness, Stanislavsky thought an actor would play a sad role more effectively.

In the 1920s, theatres in Europe and North America began to take up Stanislavsky's ideas. Not all actors and directors completely agreed with him, but the natural style of acting that he taught is now very common in Western theatre.

Konstantin Stanislavsky

# Confronting the audience

This picture shows a scene from *The Life of Galileo* by the German playwright, Bertolt Brecht

This is a scene from a play called *The Life of Galileo* by Bertolt Brecht, a German playwright. The actors are dressed in costumes which belong to the 1600s. Turn back to the previous page for a moment and compare the scene to the settings in the plays by Stanislavsky. What differences can you see?

The obvious difference is that you can immediately tell you are watching a stage performance. The actors are not standing in a room, but are on a wooden platform – their stage. Behind them hangs a backcloth, printed with a scene and artificially lit. A caption runs along the top of the backcloth, announcing the time and place that the play is set. It is not a naturalistic scene.

## Conveying a message

Unlike Stanislavsky, Brecht wanted an audience to remember that what they

Bertolt Brecht

were seeing was only a play. He saw the theatre as a way to spread a social or political message and felt the audience should be encouraged to think about the meaning behind the characters' actions, not to sympathize or identify with them. The audience could then judge the play for its message, instead of just seeing it as entertainment.

## How Brecht used the stage

The picture on the right shows a scene from another play by Brecht, called *Mother Courage and Her Children.* The actors in a Brecht play were always dressed in costumes which had been carefully researched and were correct for their period. Props, too, were authentic – look at the state of the wagon. It even has a barrel hanging from a hook on the side. These actors could really be travelling on the road and Brecht made sure the audience understood this.

However, the obvious stage surroundings would remind the audience that they were in a theatre. Lighting was always visible, and there was often a caption hung above the set before a scene was played to let the audience know what was going to happen. It was a means of making the audience distance themselves from what was shown to them on stage.

## Actors as commentators

In 1949, Brecht formed his own theatre company called the Berliner Ensemble. He used this company to experiment with his ideas. Brecht's plays were broken up with poems, music and singing, while the actors would regularly stop to comment on the actions of their character, directing these comments to the audience. This form of theatre became known as 'epic' theatre. Brecht believed all this encouraged the audience to think about the way in which the scene happened, and how things could be changed, not only on stage, but in the outside world as well.

A scene from Bertolt Brecht's *Mother Courage and Her Children*

# Acting without words

Have you ever played a party game where you have to use actions to describe something? You are not allowed to speak. Your friends have to guess from your movements and expressions what you are describing. It's not always easy to do!

## The body talks

Acting without speaking like this is usually called mime. Modern mime artists sometimes wear masks. Most important, they use movements and hand gestures to tell a story. Sometimes they use objects too. This performer is using a puppet which is almost as big as he is! Every part of a mimed performance is as carefully worked out as if there were words to learn.

A statue of a Roman mime artist

## Mime in the past

Mime has a long history. In Ancient Greece and Rome, it was linked with pantomime. Both were comic plays in which masked actors spoke as they performed various acrobatic feats. They exaggerated their movements and soon became objects of fun and ridicule for the audience. The Romans knew these plays as pantomimus. The statue pictured above shows what a Roman mime looked like. Mime also developed in different forms in Japanese Nō and Kabuki plays, and in the Kathakali plays of southern India.

This mime artist is using a life-sized puppet in his act

Modern European mime began round about 1700. It was probably started by Italian actors working in France. They could not speak French, so they developed ways of telling their stories without words. Ever since, France has been the main European home of mime. Today, many actors study mime techniques as part of their training. It is useful because it makes the actors think very carefully about their movements.

The French mime artist Marcel Marceau

## A famous mime artist

The best-known European mime artist today is a Frenchman called Marcel Marceau. You can see Marceau in this picture. He has played many different characters, but his most famous is called Bip. Bip dresses in a striped jersey and wide sailor trousers, and wears a top hat with a red rose pinned to it. His make-up is white so that the audience can see his expressions clearly. Audiences all over the world have enjoyed the antics of Bip. In 1978, Marcel Marceau set up a school to train other mime artists.

## Group mime

The characters illustrated below are pretending to pull on a long piece of rope. But there is no rope! They are miming. Why not have a go at mime with some friends. Try a 'guess and join in' activity. One of you begins a mime. It could be anything, from going for a walk on a windy day to eating an especially messy plate of food. Just remember not to speak! People join the mime as they guess what is happening. They could mime another person on the walk, or pretend to be a waiter serving food. When the mime finishes, see if all the actors agree on what they were doing.

# Famous actors

The English actor Laurence Olivier in the role of King Lear and, inset, as himself

Some actors become so famous in their lifetime that their names and faces are recognized all over the world. These pictures show a well-known English actor called Laurence Olivier, both as himself and in the part of King Lear, a character from a play by William Shakespeare.

Laurence Olivier was born in 1907. He made his first stage appearance when he was only 14 years old, in a school production of Shakespeare's *The Taming of the Shrew.* He devoted the rest of his life to acting and the theatre, and particularly to parts in Shakespeare plays. He appeared both on stage and in films, and often chose to direct as well as act. Audiences loved his daring performances, and the fact that they could never predict how he would play a part. Olivier died in 1989.

Mei Lanfang

## Mei Lanfang

Mei Lanfang, pictured here, was one of the stars of the Chinese theatre. When he was born in 1894, women did not act on the stage in China. Their parts were always taken by men. He started training when he was nine, and made his first stage appearance five years later. He was so successful at playing women's parts that he made women, for the first time, the most important characters in Chinese plays. Later, he encouraged women to train as actors.

In a series of world tours, Mei Lanfang introduced audiences in Japan, North America, Europe and Russia to the Chinese theatre. He was still acting and teaching when he died in 1961.

## Sarah Bernhardt

Sarah Bernhardt was born in France in 1844 and first appeared on stage when she was 17 years old. Unfortunately, her career began badly. Her first appearance at the national theatre company, the Comédie Française, was not a success. She had to leave the company after slapping another actor's face, but she was determined to act, and refused to give up. She was soon accepting all sorts of theatrical roles. In 1879 Sarah Bernhardt made the first of her world tours to the United States of America, Australia and Europe. By now she was famous enough to run her own theatre and choose her own roles. Despite poor health, she went on working almost until she died at the age of 79.

The French actress Sarah Bernhardt

# Learning to be an actor

These children are performing a musical called *Lollypops*

You have probably realized that acting is not a simple job – it is a skilled profession and there is a lot to learn. Most actors train for many years to learn all the aspects of playing a role, and they continue to learn each time they take on a new part. Would you like to be an actor? If so, you must be prepared for some hard work.

## Amateur groups

If you are interested in the theatre, the best way to find out more is to join an amateur group. There may be one close to where you live. Alternatively, join your school drama class, as the children in this picture have done. You'll have a lot of fun, and you will also learn what it feels like to perform on stage.

## A helping hand

Most amateur groups welcome young people who are prepared to do any jobs behind the scenes. This might include helping to paint scenery, looking after hand props or even simply pulling the curtains. This way, you will get to know what theatre life is like and whether you really enjoy it. You might decide that you want to make the theatre your career. Even if you don't, you could find an interest for your spare time that will last all your life.

## Drama school

There are many drama schools in the world where students go to learn how to act. You will have to win a place in a drama school by passing an audition. This means you will be asked to perform lines from some plays which you have learned and practised beforehand. If you pass the audition, you will be interviewed by some of the teachers at the school. They will ask you why you want to act, and what kinds of parts you would like to play. If you get into the school, you will be taught all the techniques of acting which have been discussed in this chapter, including voice production and body movement.

These student actors are learning to control their movements

## The rewards

All actors will tell you that acting is hard work. Most will also say that they wouldn't want to do any other job. There is the moment of excitement just before the curtain goes up. There is the magic of feeling that the audience is paying complete attention to your performance. At the end of the play, there is satisfaction when the curtain falls and the audience breaks into applause.

And who knows? There is the chance that one day you may be the star of the show, with your name in lights outside the theatre.

A children's theatre workshop run by the Bagamoyo College of Arts in Tanzania

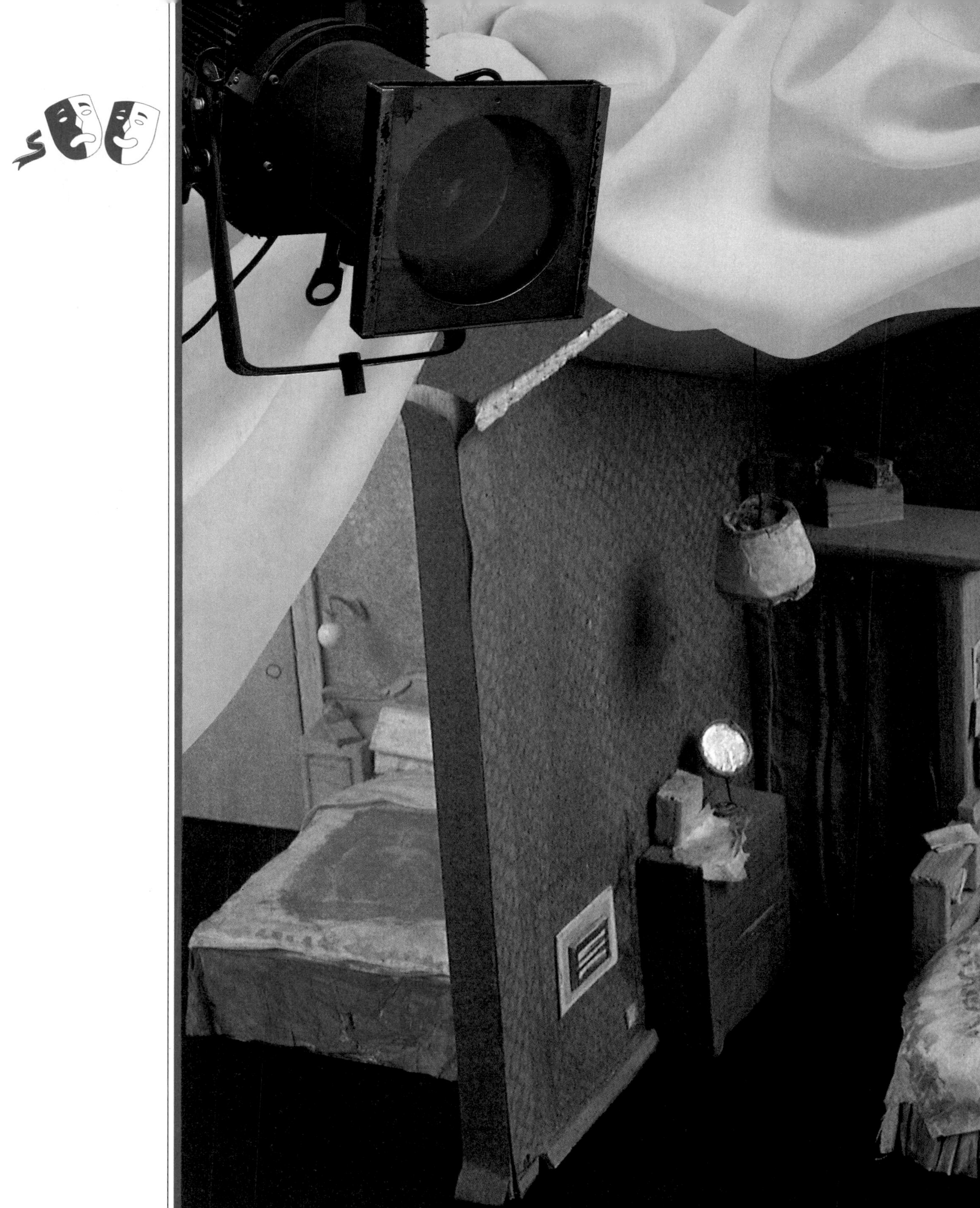

# CHAPTER FIVE

# BEHIND THE SCENES

There's a lot more to theatre than meets the eye. Come behind the scenes and find out what goes on there. In this chapter you'll learn how the design of the stage set is worked out, and how the scenery is made. You'll see how scenery is moved around, creating one new world after another. Mechanical and other devices are used to create a whole range of special effects, from storms at sea to sunsets, and from eerie ghosts to actors literally flying across the stage.

Next time you see a theatrical performance, you won't forget all the invisible effort that has gone on to make the show possible.

# Looking at the stage

The Teatro Olimpico, Italy

When you visit the theatre, do you stop to think about what goes on behind the scenes? It's not surprising if you don't, because your attention is usually held by what you can see on stage, not off it! Just look at the elaborate stage set of the theatre shown above. It is covered with pillars, statues and other carvings, which all make it look rather grand. This theatre was actually built several hundred years ago as a reconstruction of an Ancient Roman theatre. It is now one of the oldest surviving indoor theatres in the world. Through an archway, the audience could see a street stretching back into the distance. It was a clever effect. No extra scenery was needed on a stage like this.

In some theatres, you may see arches known as proscenium arches, which divide the audience from the stage. The stage is called a proscenium stage. There are many other forms of theatre design. You may watch a play presented in a theatre-in-the-round where the audience sits in a circle around the stage. Alternatively, the stage may be open, with the audience sitting in tiers on three sides.

This Peruvian festival makes use of a theatre-in-the- round stage

This lighting control board would only be used in large theatres

The design of a theatre building and its stage will always influence the way in which a production is planned. A set designer will not want to place huge pieces of scenery on a theatre-in-the-round stage, for example, because it would prevent some of the audience from seeing the actors. And on an open stage large pieces of scenery can only be placed towards the back.

## The hidden team

Hidden away, behind the scenes of every stage production, is a team of people who all contribute to the play but who are sometimes forgotten by the audience. In the larger modern theatres this team has plenty of space in which to work, using the various pieces of equipment which help to bring a performance to life. Electric stage lighting, controlled from a panel of switches and dimmers, can produce the effect of different times of day or night, as well as dazzling special effects. You can see one of these control boards in the picture above. Many theatres have multimedia equipment which can combine film or still pictures with the stage acting. They also have systems for making sound effects.

In this chapter you will read how the 'magical' effect of theatre is created – by scenery, by sound, by lighting, and much more. But it is worth remembering that not all theatres can afford sophisticated equipment, and some don't feel it is necessary anyway. Some people don't like using modern equipment because they believe it spoils the real art of acting – and that's really what the theatre is all about. Thousands of small theatre companies around the world prefer to keep to traditional, simple sets with little scenery, no special effects and no technical tricks – just good acting!

# Set design

Japanese Kabuki theatre

When the curtain rises at the beginning of a performance, the first thing you normally see on stage is the set. This may be as ordinary as three walls of a room, with doors and windows, and an arrangement of furniture. If the show is a musical or an opera, the set will be far more elaborate. There may be a painted backcloth showing some grand and historical setting, with other, smaller pieces of scenery arranged in front of it. There may even be buildings, or parts of buildings, to the side of the stage. Of course there may also be very little, or even no scenery at all, as in classical Chinese and Japanese theatre. A fir tree painted onto a backcloth traditionally provides a simple setting for Japanese Kabuki theatre.

## The first step

A set designer may have lots of exciting ideas for creating a new set but may find it's difficult to put them into practice. The first big problem will be money. How much is available? Then there is the question of space. Is the stage large enough for bulky pieces of scenery? How many actors are in the production and how will they move around? Do they need space to dance? Will it be useful to have steps and balconies on stage, to give height to the set? There are many questions to consider.

Once set designers have a good idea of what is needed, they usually build a scale model of the proposed set. This avoids costly mistakes because it is much easier and cheaper to make changes to a model than to the completed set.

This picture shows a set designer and stage director discussing a model set

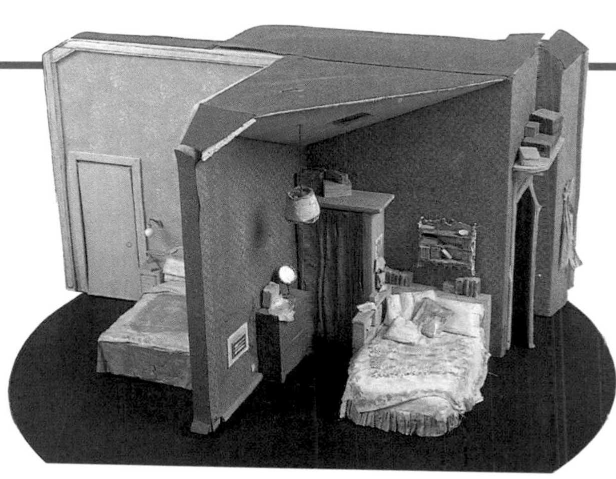

This model set was made by an English set designer called Alan Tagg

## A revolving stage

In some theatres, part of the stage is built from a huge revolving circular platform. This allows two or three different sets to be constructed back to back. The platform can then be rotated to change the scene between the acts of a play. You can see a model above that was designed for a theatre with a revolving stage. It holds three sets, although you can only see two of them.

## An underwater setting

Why not design and build your own model set? You could choose any scene from your favourite book, or follow the suggestions for making the underwater set shown here. First, cut three holes into the sides and front of a sturdy cardboard box. Cut a piece of white card to fit the back of the box and paint this with an underwater scene to form a moveable backdrop.

Next make the side scenery, or wings, from painted card. Cut the card into different shapes. Attach these wings to sticks with sticky tape so they can be dropped down into position as shown. Hang strips of green ribbon or tissue paper from another stick to form seaweed. You might like to use sandpaper to make a sandy sea floor, and you could also add a few shells. Turn to page 182 to find out how you can use your model set to put on a miniature play.

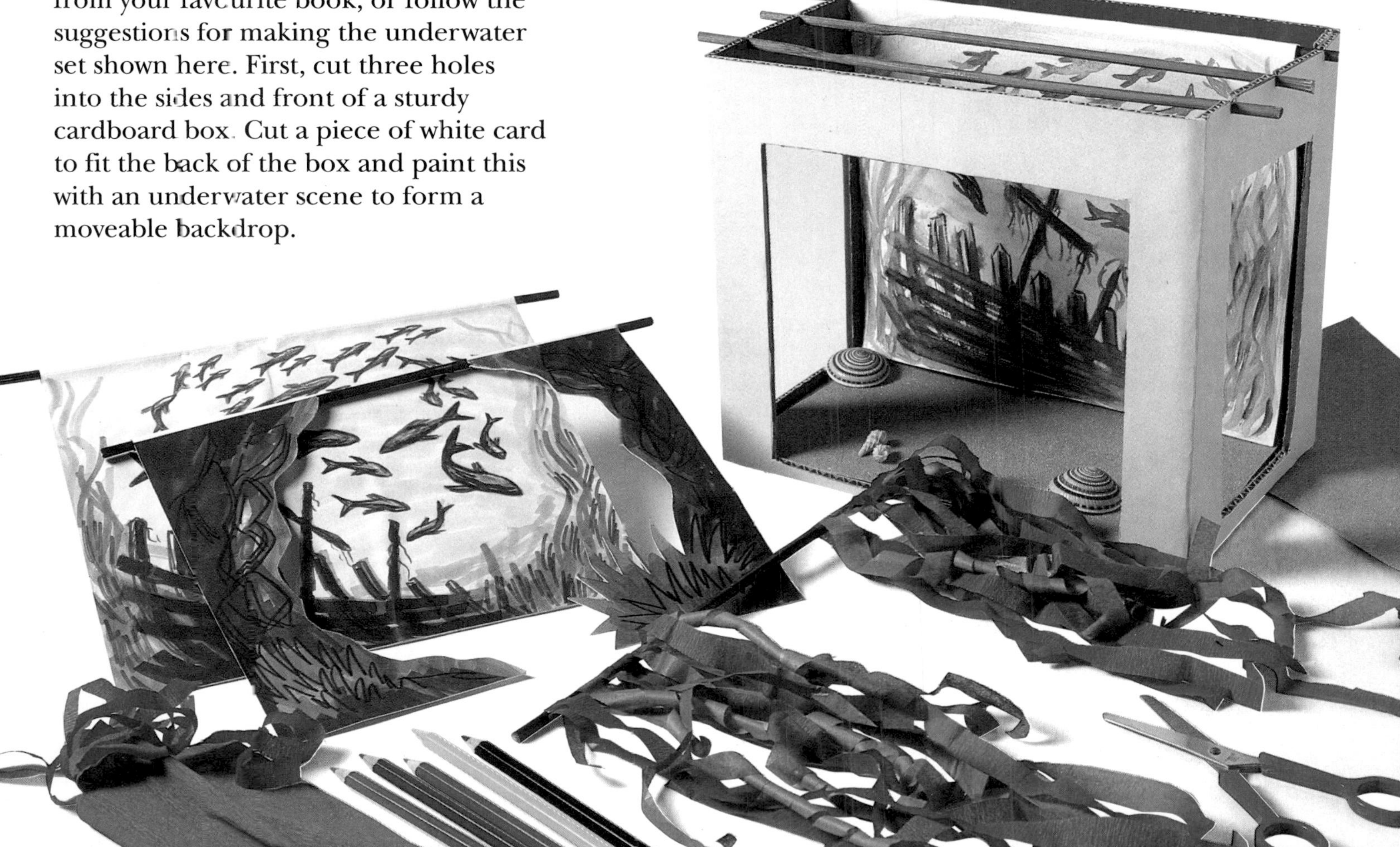

# Building and moving scenery

These stagehands are constructing a huge staircase

Most scenery is made up of wooden frames covered with painted canvas or hardboard. These are called flats. Flats are supported from behind by wooden or metal struts, and held together with clamps. Similar frames are used to make long, low pieces of scenery, such as hedges or low walls, which are positioned part-way down the stage. You can see this kind of framework in the picture of a stage staircase. Can you see how the staircase has been supported on small metal wheels? This makes it easily moveable.

## Flats

If you had watched the spectacular scene below appear on stage, you would have found it an almost magical transformation. Some 350 years ago, an Italian stage designer called Giacomo Torelli invented a new system of moving scenery. Instead of resting on the stage, his flats passed through grooves and were fixed onto rollers beneath. In this way, the flats could be quickly and smoothly changed. His invention led to

The stage setting for this production was designed by an Italian called Giacomo Torelli in the 1600s

extraordinary effects, bringing realistic storms, waterfalls and avalanches onto the stage. Many people went to the theatre in the 1600s to enjoy the effects as much as to enjoy the acting!

## Large-scale scenery

When a play is staged out of doors, the director often makes use of natural scenery – a wall or a tree. But inside a theatre building, all the scenery has to be man-made. This picture shows the construction of a life-size tree for a stage performance. Very few theatre companies have workshops this big, but it is fascinating to see something on this grand scale. How do you think the tree is made? It is built up on a wire and wood framework. When it is has been moulded, it will be painted. On stage, it will look just like a living tree.

This tree is being made in the workshops of the Welsh National Opera

## Model a palm tree

Large pieces of scenery, such as the tree trunk being built in the picture above, are made in model form first to fit a model set. You might like to try making the model palm tree shown here. If you make the model set shown on the previous page, you could use the palm tree to change it into a tropical island.

You will need stiff brown card for the trunk. Cut out four quarter-circles, making these progressively larger in size. Cut frills along the curved edges, then form them into cones. Fit these cones inside each other to build up a trunk. To make your leaves, roll up a piece of green card, then cut into one end as shown on the opposite page. Stick the other end into the top of the trunk.

# Machinery and magic

This picture shows how Pepper's Ghost was thrown onto the stage

The audience watch enthralled as a ghostly figure appears on stage. One of the actors lunges with a sword, but the sword passes straight through the ghost and the apparition continues to walk across the stage!

If you had sat in a European theatre in the late 1800s, this was one of the many special effects you might have seen. The ghost was known as Pepper's Ghost after the first person to use it in the theatre, John Henry Pepper. So how did it work? An actor dressed as a ghost stood in the orchestra pit. A light threw his reflection onto a sheet of glass which was placed at the front of the stage – and the audience saw this reflection as a phantom figure. This ghostly method is not used today. Ghost effects are produced by shining a light through a thin material called gauze, which is hung at the front of the stage.

## Special effects

Playwrights and stage designers have always been inventive in thinking up ways of making plays more exciting. The Ancient Greeks used a kind of crane to lower actors playing gods to the stage. Similar machines were widely used to lower painted clouds into position or to allow costumed actors — perhaps fairies or spirits – to make a 'flying' entrance. Plays of the 1800s often included scenes of 'trickwork', using trap doors like the one below, overhead wires and pulleys, and other special gadgets.

This clown is raised onto the stage through a trap door

## Horses on stage

This print was published in a newspaper in 1902. It is a scene from a spectacular stage performance called *Ben-Hur* in which there is a thrilling chariot race. This theatre found a good way of using live horses rather than dummies. Look how each team of horses is galloping on a wooden treadmill which stops them from moving forward.

The cutaway diagram shows the machinery which was built to operate the treadmills. The scenery behind, showing spectators in an arena, was made to move in the opposite direction to make the horses look as if they were galloping even faster. It was a clever illusion. Can you imagine how noisy it must have been?

This performance of *Ben-Hur* took place in 1902

## Powdered blood

Have you ever watched a sword fight take place on stage? If you have, you probably saw blood spill onto the loser's shirt. This is not real blood, of course. It is a special effect. In the past, a blood-filled animal bladder was hidden under an actor's costume, and when it was pierced, out gushed the blood! Fake blood can now be bought in liquid form or in capsules. The capsules are used for blood appearing from an actor's mouth. They melt in the mouth and the harmless powder mixes with saliva to form realistic blood.

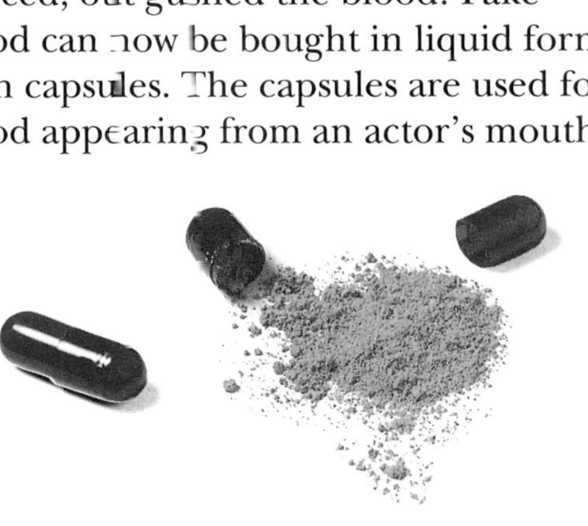

# From candles to electricity

This oil lamp is used in shadow-puppet performances

Lighting is a crucial part of any stage performance. Lighting techniques can keep a section of the stage in shadow. Key characters can be spotlit when they speak, and other characters kept completely in the dark. Different coloured gels can be put in front of the lights to create a certain mood or atmosphere. In fact, lighting has become so important in the theatre that when a theatre is closed, actors talk about it being 'dark'.

But for many thousands of years, plays were only performed outside and in daylight, or they were lit by torchlight, firelight or by oil lamps. Star performers in Japanese Kabuki plays often had to act while a candle balanced at the end of a pole was held up to their face!

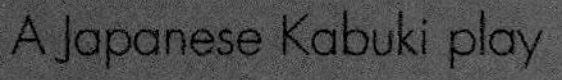
A Japanese Kabuki play

Sometimes plays today are performed with these same means of lighting – and it works well. The firelight in the performance of a Japanese Kabuki play casts a warm glow over the actors on stage. Oil lamps are traditionally used in Indonesian shadow-puppet shows.

## Candles and gaslight

About 300 years ago, when plays began to be performed in permanent indoor theatres, stage directors had to look for ways of fixing lighting over the stage. Candles were an easy choice. Candelabra were hung over the actors while candle footlights were arranged along the front of the stage, rather like the candles at the bottom of this page. Theatres later added candles at the sides of the stage and above it, using mirrors to increase the light by reflection.

But candlelight was by no means perfect. The amount of light given out by a candle can't be controlled. Candles can't be dimmed or made to look brighter. This problem was solved by the discovery of gaslight in 1815 because the gas jets could be turned up or down. One theatre in London, England, employed 30 gasmen to control the light during a performance.

## In the limelight

Another new invention was limelight. This was produced by burning lime in a jet of gas. Limelight was used to throw a bright light onto the principal actor in a scene. We still talk today about someone being 'in the limelight', although limelight is no longer used.

## The danger of fire

Candles, gaslight and limelight were all extremely dangerous. Hundreds of theatres burned down in the 1700s and 1800s after flames caught hold of curtains and scenery. The worst ever theatre disaster was in 1845 in China, where over 1,600 people died in a theatre blaze. It was clear that a new and safe method of lighting was badly needed.

## Enter electricity

In 1879, an American scientist called Thomas Alva Edison invented the electric lamp. Electric light has no naked flame, so it was much safer than previous forms of lighting. It was also much brighter than gaslight, and much easier to control. In the same year, the California Theatre in San Francisco, in the United States of America, became the first theatre in the world to install electric lighting. Two years later, the newly-opened Savoy Theatre in London became the first electrically-lit theatre in Europe. A new chapter in the history of the theatre had started.

# Stage lighting today

Light effects on stage for a performance of *Song and Dance*

The stage in this picture is flooded with light. It streams down from hundreds of lamps, all controlled by just one operator sitting at a computer. Lighting designers use the lamps to create the mood of the show. They can move the lights around, focusing the beams from several directions in order to avoid ugly shadows. They can dim them gradually with sliding knobs called faders. Good lighting can bring out the best in the set and the actors.

## Theatre lamps and their effects

Although we still use the word footlights when we talk about the theatre, footlights are no longer used to light the stage. Today, the lighting comes from powerful floodlights and spotlights placed on rungs high above the actors. These lights can pivot around, shedding light everywhere or just on one small piece of action.

Transparent painted disks called effect heads can be attached to the front of a spotlight. These are used to provide sophisticated special effects, such as flickering firelight, or ripples in a lake. Lights can also be used to create effects such as a dramatic streak of lightning or an explosion. Gobos are specially-cut sheets of aluminium which are used in a similar way to effect heads to cast shadows onto the stage. Coloured filters called gels are used to change the colour of the light.

## The effects on actors

In the days when the main lighting came from the front of the stage, actors had to stay upstage – that is, towards the back where the lights shone. If they came too far forward, they found themselves in shadow. Now that the whole stage can be brightly lit, actors can use the stage area to the full

Modern lighting is brighter, too. The exaggerated style of acting that was popular 100 years ago came about partly because, in dim lighting, the actors' faces couldn't be seen clearly. They had

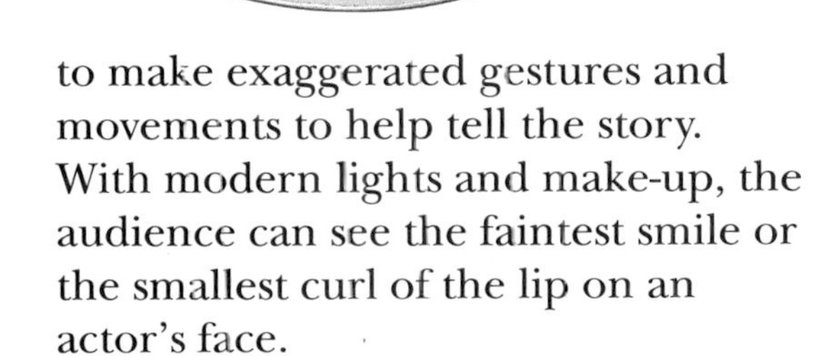

to make exaggerated gestures and movements to help tell the story. With modern lights and make-up, the audience can see the faintest smile or the smallest curl of the lip on an actor's face.

## Make a colour wheel

You can see the effects of coloured filters and lighting for yourself by making a colour wheel. You need to flatten a round tin foil dish. You may find it easier to cut off the rim first. Cut three circles into this dish and cover them with coloured transparent sweet papers. You can attach these to the foil with sticky tape. Now use a split pin to attach your colour wheel to a piece of card. Use a torch behind the colour wheel and watch the colours change as you turn the wheel. You could use this with a toy theatre, described on page 113, if you want to put on a miniature show.

# Sound effects

This man has a range of instruments and equipment to produce some special sound effects

The scene is taking place during a heavy storm. Thunder crashes overhead and raindrops drum on the roof. Suddenly there is a loud bang – a gunshot. Horse's hooves can be heard thundering past, loud at first, then receding into the distance...

In the theatre, such dramatic scenes are brought to life with the clever use of sound effects. These may include doorbells, footsteps, gunshots, thunder, the ringing of telephones, and any other sounds which help to keep the audience's interest. Today, many theatres use tape-recorded sound, but a lot of small theatre companies still make their own 'live' sound effects. That means that the sounds are produced on stage, with a microphone to carry them to the audience.

## A storm is brewing

Let's go back to the heavy storm. How would you produce the necessary sounds? The rumble of thunder can be made by shaking a 'thunder sheet' of thin, flexible metal. The more the metal is wobbled, the louder the sound it produces. You can do this at home with a large sheet of thin card. What about the pitter-patter of raindrops? Try dropping grains of rice slowly onto a metal dish, or spraying water into a bucket. It's easy and very effective.

But stop a minute! The director calls for a stronger rain sound – more like hail. How would you do this? Think about the sound. It is a hard drumming. Shake some dried peas about in a wooden box, and you will come very close. Does your storm sound realistic? There's one thing missing – wind.

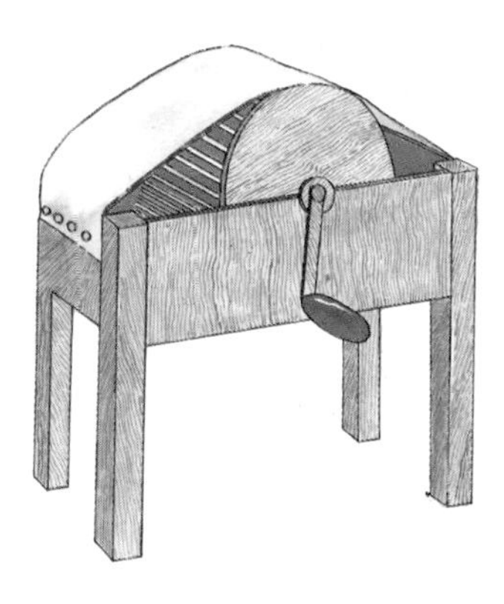

The sound of the wind is difficult to reproduce without a special wind machine. This produces a realistic noise as a wooden drum revolves against a silk screen. At home, you could try blowing and whistling down a long cardboard tube. Finally you will have to add the gunshot – perhaps the clack of two sticks of wood – and the hoofbeats. The sound of a galloping horse is traditionally made by clattering together two halves of a coconut shell, or by banging them on a hard surface. Producing the sounds for just one short scene certainly takes a lot of thought!

Not all theatres use methods like these. In Japanese Kabuki theatre a drum is beaten to suggest different weather conditions, from wind and rain to snow and hail. In Kabuki, the method is not so very important. What matters is that the sound occurs at the right time.

## The timing of sound effects

"There's the doorbell," says the actor, "I'll get it." "What doorbell?" thinks the audience, who haven't heard a sound. Then a bell rings, and the audience erupts with laughter. Sound effects are no good at all unless they are timed correctly. Actors need them to use as cues for their next lines. But good timing is also essential if the audience is to believe in the play. Obviously the person in charge of sound effects is very important and must follow a cue sheet which indicates exactly when each noise has to be made.

# Costume

These actors are dressed as frogs for a special dance-drama in Bali

The actors in the performance pictured above are all dressed in special costumes. Can you tell what the three in animal costumes are supposed to be? They are frogs. By wearing costumes, the actors lead an audience into the imaginary world they are trying to create. Costume helps the audience to recognize the part that the actor is playing. And it helps actors to play their parts convincingly. This is true even if the play is set in modern times and the actors wear everyday clothes.

This theatre group are discussing costume designs

## Designing costumes

You can see examples of costume sketches below. Look how a material sample has been pinned to each sketch. Designing and making costumes for the theatre is a specialized kind of dressmaking. The clothes are often hand-sewn, or at least the finishing touches and final alterations are made by hand. Costume designers must keep in mind what actions an actor will be required to make while wearing the costume. Look back at how loose the frog costumes are, allowing the actors inside to bend and move quite freely as they make their frog-like leaps.

A costume designer also has to remember that the actors may have only a few minutes to change from one costume to another. They won't have a lot of time to undo rows and rows of buttons. Fastenings must be quick and easy to manage. All these things are taken into account when the design sketches are discussed.

Some theatre companies, such as those of the Chinese and Japanese traditional theatre, have their own stocks of costumes which they use until they are worn out. Others go to hire firms. But for new productions the costumes have to be specially made.

This man is ironing costumes for a Peking Opera performance

## Looking after costumes

The man pictured above has a lot of ironing to do! He is part of a team looking after costumes for the Peking Opera in China. Costumes have to be carefully checked between performances of any play. If an actor stumbles on stage and the costume is torn, it will have to be speedily repaired and cleaned before the next performance. So after a performance ends and the actors and audience have gone home, the work of the costume department goes on.

Three costume design sketches

# Building a new face

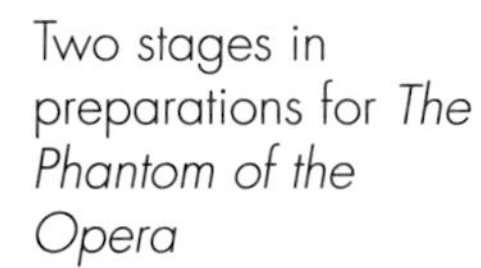

Two stages in preparations for *The Phantom of the Opera*

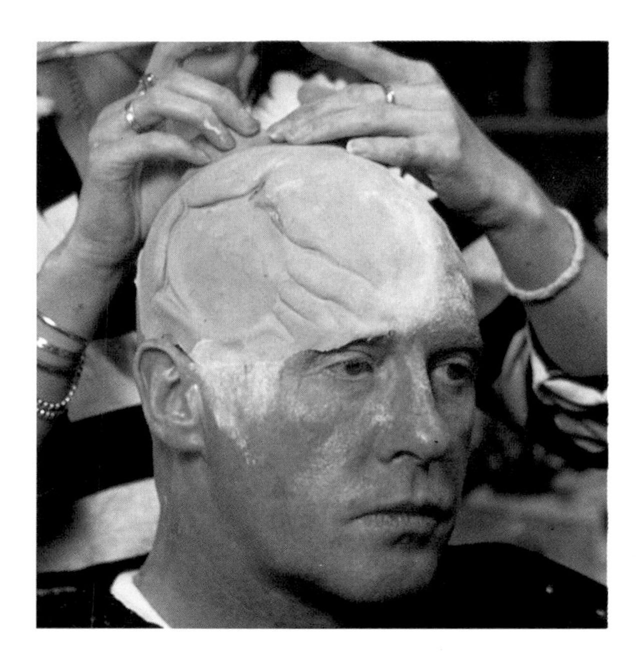

Sometimes an actor has to undergo a complete transformation! Perhaps a horrific accident has left terrible scars on the face of the character he is playing. The pictures on this page show the English actor Michael Crawford being prepared for his role in a stage version of *The Phantom of the Opera*. The make-up is so heavy that in the second picture the actor's own face has almost disappeared! Deep scars cover his face, and his mouth looks badly misshapen. A thick layer of make-up even covers his neck.

Creating a new appearance like the one required for the phantom is not easy. It takes about two hours. The false face you can see is made of a rubbery foam latex which is stuck to the skin with a special glue called spirit gum. The features on the face can then be painted on to the latex.

The actor's real hair has been covered up and in the second picture you can see a wig is being added. This wig is held together on a fine gauze, the edges of which will need to be hidden under yet another layer of make-up. Michael Crawford had to have his face prepared in this way for six performances a week. Just imagine how patient he had to be.

*Spirit gum*

*Liquid latex*

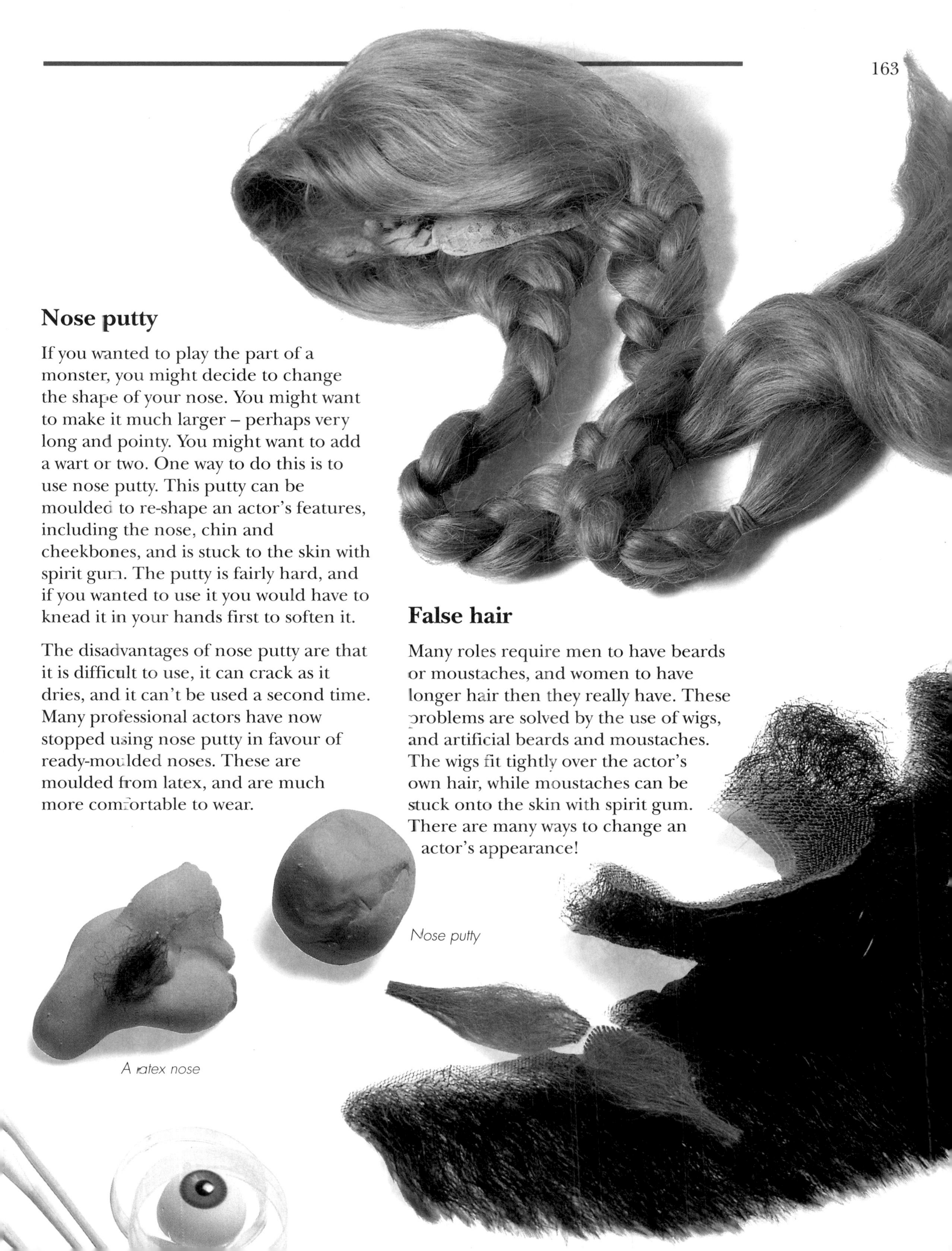

## Nose putty

If you wanted to play the part of a monster, you might decide to change the shape of your nose. You might want to make it much larger – perhaps very long and pointy. You might want to add a wart or two. One way to do this is to use nose putty. This putty can be moulded to re-shape an actor's features, including the nose, chin and cheekbones, and is stuck to the skin with spirit gum. The putty is fairly hard, and if you wanted to use it you would have to knead it in your hands first to soften it.

The disadvantages of nose putty are that it is difficult to use, it can crack as it dries, and it can't be used a second time. Many professional actors have now stopped using nose putty in favour of ready-moulded noses. These are moulded from latex, and are much more comfortable to wear.

## False hair

Many roles require men to have beards or moustaches, and women to have longer hair then they really have. These problems are solved by the use of wigs, and artificial beards and moustaches. The wigs fit tightly over the actor's own hair, while moustaches can be stuck onto the skin with spirit gum. There are many ways to change an actor's appearance!

*Nose putty*

*A latex nose*

# Bringing in the audience

These actors are performing to a tiny audience

These spectators are waiting for a street carnival procession

Everything is ready. The performers are in costume and they have rehearsed their lines. The scenery and props are in place. The director calls for the curtain to be lifted – and the actors peer out at an empty theatre.

This disastrous scene is one which performers and theatres try to avoid. It makes a sad picture, as you can see on the left. Compare this with the cheerful, colourful crowd awaiting a carnival procession in Madrid, Spain. They form an important part of the spectacle. Performers need an audience.

## The need for publicity

People won't come to see a show unless they know about it. They also have to be persuaded that it is worth seeing, especially if they have to pay for a seat. This involves publicity. Everybody connected with a show knows that if they want people to turn up, the show has to be written about and talked about in as many different places as possible, and as often as possible. Without publicity, there will be no audience.

## Publicity in action

As soon as the details of a play have been arranged, the publicity team gets to work. Newspapers are good places for announcing forthcoming events, and local papers will often help promote local theatrical events in return for a couple of free seats. The people who use these free seats are called critics, and they will write a review of the first performance.

A critic's review usually discusses the play itself – whether or not it has a strong plot – the stage set and costumes, and the actors' performances. No one thinks that the critics will be kind about the show just because they have free seats. But if, as the theatre hopes, it is a good review this might encourage people to come along to later performances.

Most theatre companies also produce carefully designed posters. These usually feature an eye-catching scene from the play to give some idea of what it's all about – the fierce warriors pictured here decorate a Japanese poster. Photographs of the leading actors will also be displayed outside the theatre and sent to local newspapers and magazines. The actors might be interviewed for a feature on local television or radio. The aim is to make sure that everyone who is likely to be interested in the show hears about it.

A Japanese theatre poster

# CHAPTER SIX

# ON STAGE

Putting on a play requires a lot of hard work from everyone involved. In this chapter, you can find out how the actors practise their performance again and again until it's right. You'll realize how important the director is in organizing everyone on stage, and making sure that they work as a team.

You can be a director, too, and organize your own show. You may like to put on a play you've written yourself. You could use a toy theatre, or get together with a group of friends. You'll find that your final performance will be well worth all your hard work.

# Writing a play

History, myth, legend, adventure ... there's no end to the list of subjects people write plays about. Some writers are interested in everyday happenings, while others may want to create a dream-world far away from real life.

In this book you have read about many different types of play. Why not try writing a play of your own? You could take the idea from a favourite book. But don't try to turn the whole book into a play. Instead, choose one of the most exciting incidents of the story and try writing it as a play that lasts about 10 or 15 minutes.

## The first steps

Writing a play is very similar to writing a story, as long as you bear in mind some simple rules. First, remember that you can only tell the story through the words spoken by the characters. You can't write descriptions or explanations. So from an early point in your script, you have to write lines for your actors that will make their characterization clear to the audience. Think also about how many characters you would like. Don't introduce too many for your first play – perhaps three or four.

## From the beginning

Like any story, a play must have a beginning, a middle and an end. The beginning sets the scene and introduces the characters. Your audience will ask themselves, "Who are these people and what are they doing?" The beginning of the play must answer those questions. The middle is the heart of the story. If you write a mystery or suspense this is when the audience will be asking, "What's the problem?" The next question is, "How are they going to solve it?" The last part of the play provides the answer. Of course, when you have had some experience at writing, you can change this order. Some plays begin with a dramatic event which leaves many unanswered questions. This means that the scene has to be set and the characters introduced at a later stage. When you are writing, you are the boss – you are in control of what happens.

## The fun of action

Always include some action, such as a mock fight or a chase. If you can, give the audience some surprises. You could make hidden characters jump out from behind curtains, for example. Make these events simple. It is easy enough to write about a spectacular event like an erupting volcano, but how could you possibly show this on stage? If your ideas are too wild, you may find you can't transfer them to the stage.

## Listen to others

Don't be afraid to rewrite again and again until you're really happy with your effort. Most playwrights do this! You might find it helpful to ask someone else to read through your script – they will probably make some good suggestions which will improve your text. In fact, professional actors often ask for small changes to their lines to make them easier to say. Or they may feel a change will explain the story better. Listening to different opinions about a text can be valuable.

Once you're happy with your text, it's time to prepare for the performance.

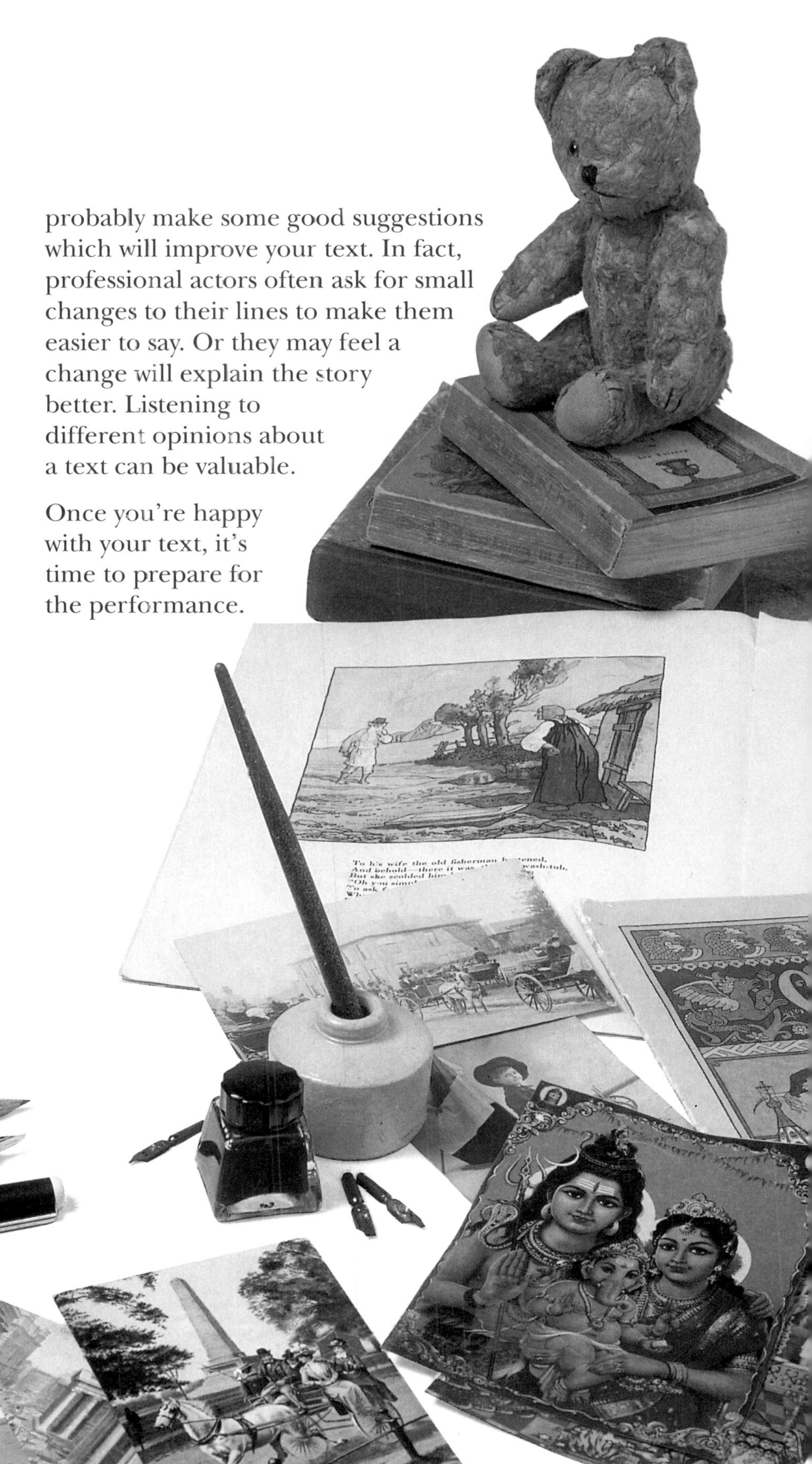

# Preparing for a performance

Backstage preparations in a theatre in the 1800s

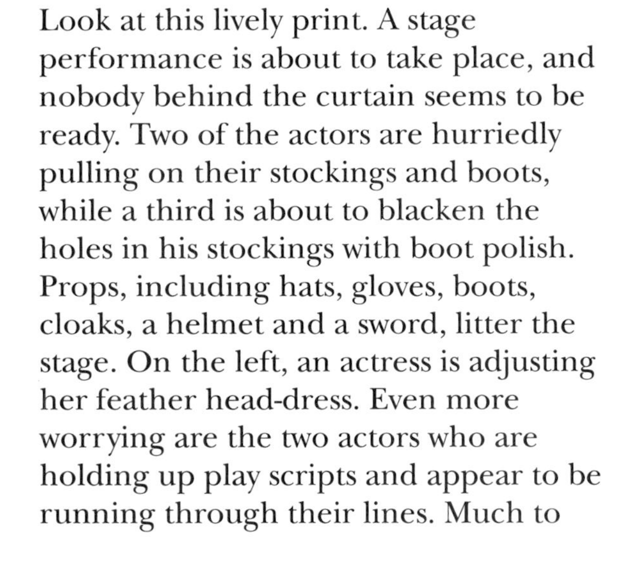

Look at this lively print. A stage performance is about to take place, and nobody behind the curtain seems to be ready. Two of the actors are hurriedly pulling on their stockings and boots, while a third is about to blacken the holes in his stockings with boot polish. Props, including hats, gloves, boots, cloaks, a helmet and a sword, litter the stage. On the left, an actress is adjusting her feather head-dress. Even more worrying are the two actors who are holding up play scripts and appear to be running through their lines. Much to their dismay, the grinning stagehand is raising the curtain. The scene is one of utter chaos!

The print provides a fascinating glimpse of backstage preparations for a play in an English theatre in the early 1800s. Of course, if the members of a cast were this disorganized, the play would never take place. But the picture is still interesting because it shows almost every stage in an actor's preparation for a performance.

This Japanese actor is reading from a scroll

## Learning lines

When the actors receive their scripts, the first thing they have to do is learn their lines. They usually do this by saying the lines over and over again, until they are quite sure they can remember them. This picture shows a Japanese actor in the 1700s. He appears to be having a quick peek at his script, perhaps to remind himself of his lines. Learning lines is not an easy task. The actors not only have to remember the words, they also have to think about the way to say them if they are to give a convincing performance.

## Don't forget!

Even after careful preparation, actors do sometimes forget their lines. This is something every actor dreads. But just in case the worst happens, there is usually a prompter to help out. A prompter has the job of reading through the play as it's being acted on stage, and whispering the right words to the actors if they lose their place.

Prompters are hidden from the audience. The one in this picture is looking up from a hole in the front of the stage. A shield hides her from the audience. The prompter has to concentrate on every line and be aware all the time of what is coming next. If she loses concentration for just a short time and an actor forgets a line, there will be an obvious pause in the play.

A prompter in her box

# Directing a play

How many people can you see on the stage in this opera performance? It's not easy to count – the performers are huddled together in a crowd. In fact there were at least 1,000 performers involved in this production of *Aida*, by the Italian composer Verdi. The performance took place in Egypt in 1987. How do you think the members of this enormous cast know what to do, and where to stand?

## Organizing the team

The actors themselves can't possibly see how they look on stage. Someone else has to organize the performers, to make sure they know what to do and when to do it. And that's the important job of the director. A director is like the manager of the theatrical team.

## From paper to stage

First of all, the director is given the script, or words, of the play that is going to be performed. It could be a new play written by a living writer, or it may have been written a long time ago. The director then has to find the best way of bringing the writer's words to life on the stage.

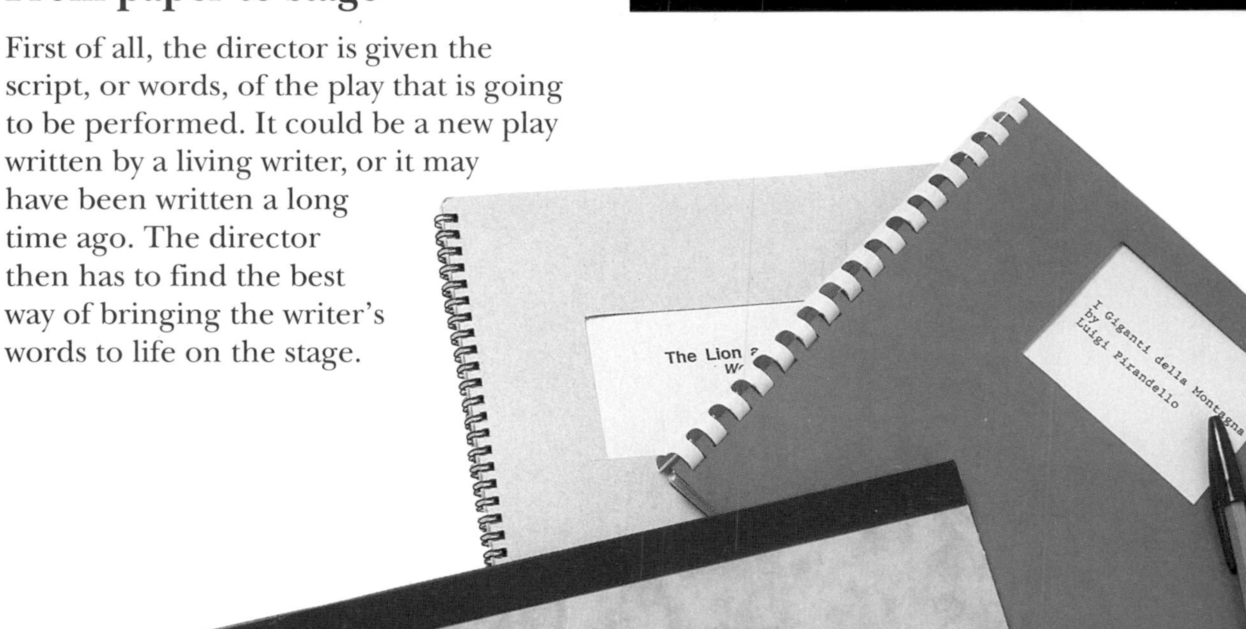

A performance of Verdi's opera, *Aida*

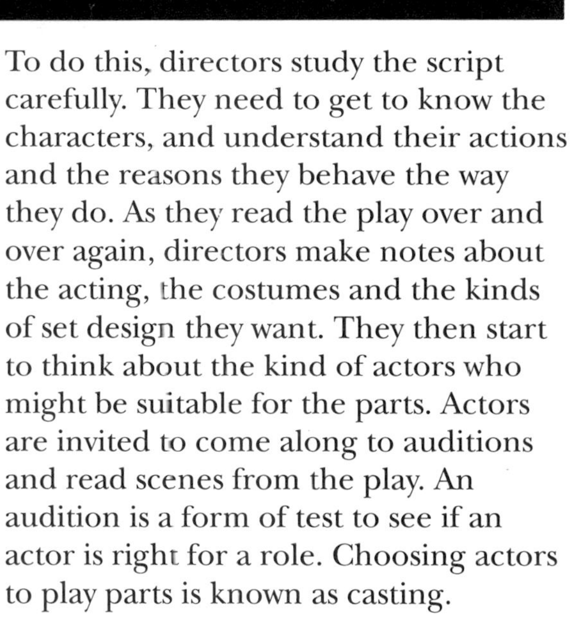

To do this, directors study the script carefully. They need to get to know the characters, and understand their actions and the reasons they behave the way they do. As they read the play over and over again, directors make notes about the acting, the costumes and the kinds of set design they want. They then start to think about the kind of actors who might be suitable for the parts. Actors are invited to come along to auditions and read scenes from the play. An audition is a form of test to see if an actor is right for a role. Choosing actors to play parts is known as casting.

## Moving on to the rehearsals

Once the parts are cast, the director begins to hold practice sessions, or rehearsals. This picture shows an early rehearsal. The director is standing on the right. He is running through one scene of the play with some of the actors. They are not yet in costume, but have a few props on the table in front of them. Behind these principal actors you can see others, who may not be in this particular scene, but need to know what is going on. You can read more about rehearsals on pages 176 and 177.

This director is holding a first rehearsal

# Acting and directing

Some years ago, acting and directing were considered to be two parts of the same job. They were not separated. When Zeami Motokiyo founded the Japanese Nō theatre 600 years ago, he wrote the plays, took the leading parts and also directed them. In China, too, the 'head actor', who was usually the most experienced, often wrote, directed and acted in the same play.

The French playwright Molière, born in 1622, was another writer-actor-director with his own company of actors. He specialized in comedy and became a great favourite of King Louis XIV of France. Molière's plays were performed at the royal palace at Versailles, and the king's friendship made Molière famous and fashionable. Between 1658 and 1673 he wrote, directed and acted in at least one new play a year, and sometimes two or three. Molière is pictured here.

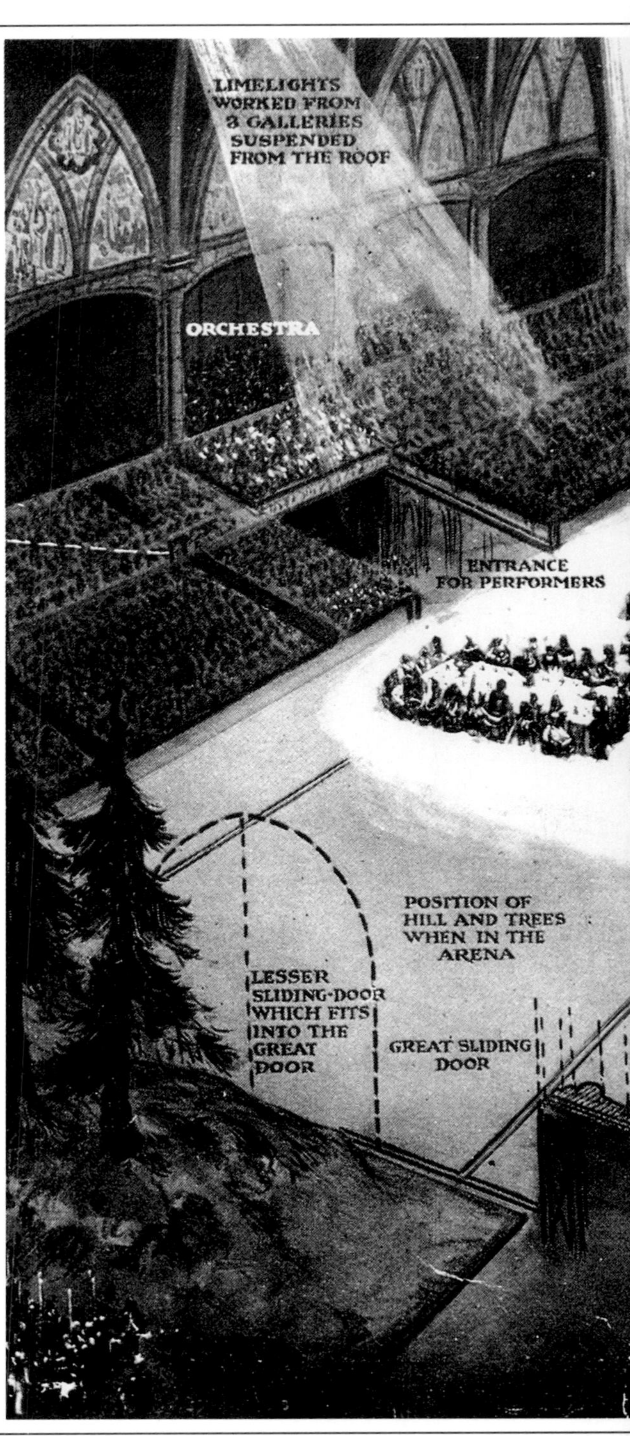

## A new departure

The split between the jobs of acting and directing first happened about 100 years ago. One of the first directors – as opposed to actor-directors – was an Austrian called Max Reinhardt. Reinhardt started his career as an actor, but soon became more interested in the way plays were staged than in acting in them. In 1903 he gave up acting to pursue a career as a director.

Max Reinhardt

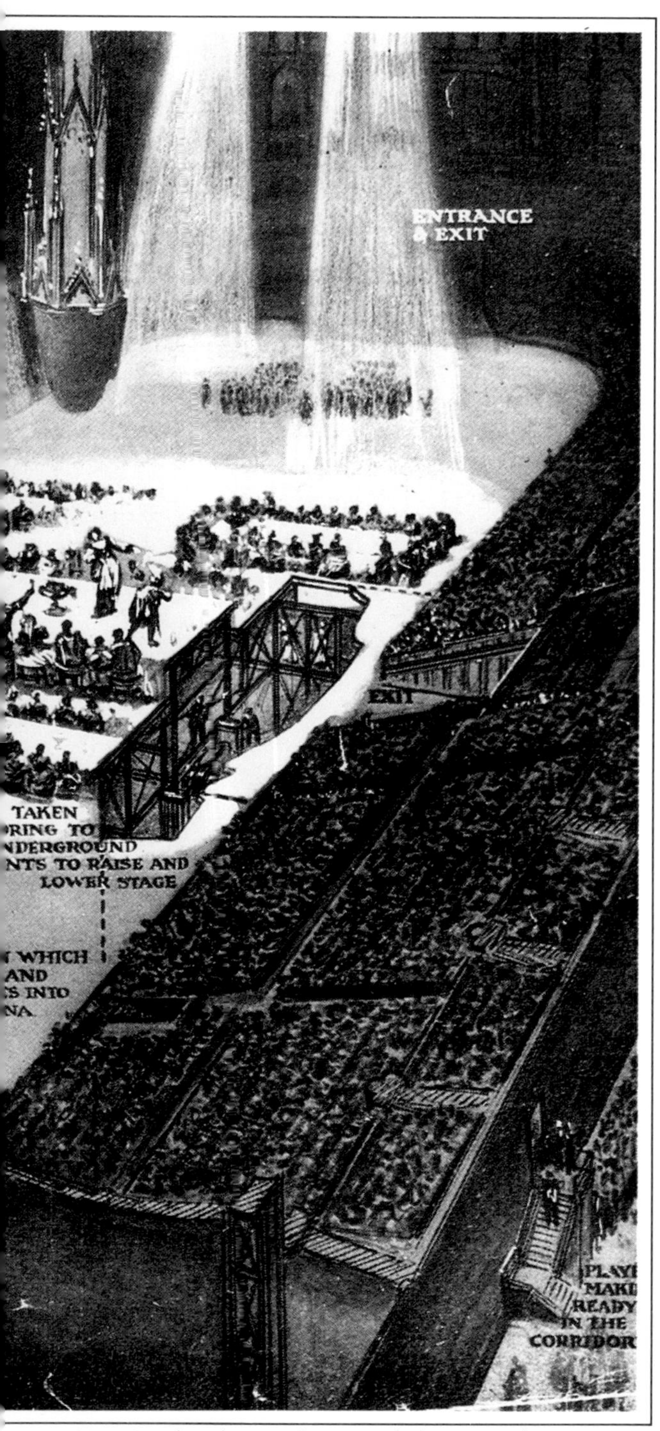


Max Reinhardt's production of The Miracle was staged in 1911 in London, England

Reinhardt became famous all over Europe for his spectacular productions involving huge crowd scenes. Ordinary theatres were too small for these events. So where do you think they were staged? Most were put on in market places, cathedral squares and exhibition halls. This picture shows one of Reinhardt's most famous productions, *The Miracle*. Look at the walls. *The Miracle* was staged in an exhibition hall but you can see how the walls have been cleverly altered so that they look like those of a cathedral.

## An actor-director today

Many writers still direct and act in their own plays. One of the founders of modern theatre in Singapore is Kuo Pao Kun, who trained as an actor in Australia. He began writing plays in two of Singapore's official languages, Chinese and English, but soon found there was a shortage of actors in these languages. So he started his own school to train actors to perform his plays. His shows combined the ancient traditions of China and the modern techniques of the Western world.

# The rehearsal

What do you think the actors in this picture are doing? There's a collection of objects lying at their feet. Do you think these are the props? And there's a length of material stretched out behind them. Could that be part of the scenery? Perhaps they have met to practise a play that they will be performing soon. This practising is known as the rehearsal.

These actors are rehearsing in the Cameroon

## Starting off

At the first rehearsals of a play, the actors run through the scenes, with the director supervising the action. They also sort out the props they need. The actors will already have begun to learn their lines, though they may not yet be word-perfect. If the play is based on historical events, some of the actors might read up about the period concerned to get to know a bit more about life at that time. This can help them to understand why their characters behave the way they do.

A performance of *The Wizard of Oz*

These actors are rehearsing for *The Wizard of Oz*

## From rehearsal to stage

Look at these two pictures. The black-and-white photograph shows a group of actors wearing their own clothes and no wigs or make-up. The second picture shows the same actors on stage in full costume. At first glance there is a big difference between the two pictures. But apart from the costumes, is there really such a difference? Let's take a closer look.

The pictures show a rehearsal and stage performance of a children's musical called *The Wizard of Oz*. This musical brings together four characters – a tin man, a lion, a scarecrow, and a girl called Dorothy. Each one of them is in search of something new, and to find it they have to follow a yellow brick road.

## Creating the mood

What similarities can you see between the pictures? The line-up of actors is the same – they are even accompanied by the dog in their rehearsal! Now look at what they're doing. They are in a large, empty hall. They're striding down an imaginary yellow brick road. It doesn't matter that there isn't really a yellow brick road, because they have already started to think themselves into their roles. Look how the actor playing the lion is using his hands as paws, while the tin man is carrying his axe and the scarecrow is wearing a hat. You can see that the actor's imagination is very important in creating the right feeling of the play.

# A total transformation!

1. Attaching the snout

2. Highlighting the eyes and chin

3. Sponging dark brown over the rest of the face

4. Adding details of the eye make-up

5. Painting the nose

Have you ever pretended to be a rabbit, or a cat, or even a lion? Skilful make-up can transform your face into any one of these creatures – and many more! These pictures show you the stages involved in turning this young actress into a lion.

## From nose to snout

A lion has a snout which is very different from a human nose. In the theatre, this problem is overcome by the use of a snout moulded from latex. A mould like this is called a prosthetic. Once the girl's face has been cleansed, the make-up artist attaches the prosthetic using a harmless glue called spirit gum. The spirit gum is spread around the top edges of the prosthetic only – if the bottom were stuck it would be hard for the girl to speak!

1. Adding yellow streaks of fur

2. Black whiskers and red lips complete the effect

3. The end result

4. Detail of the eye

5. Detail of the snout

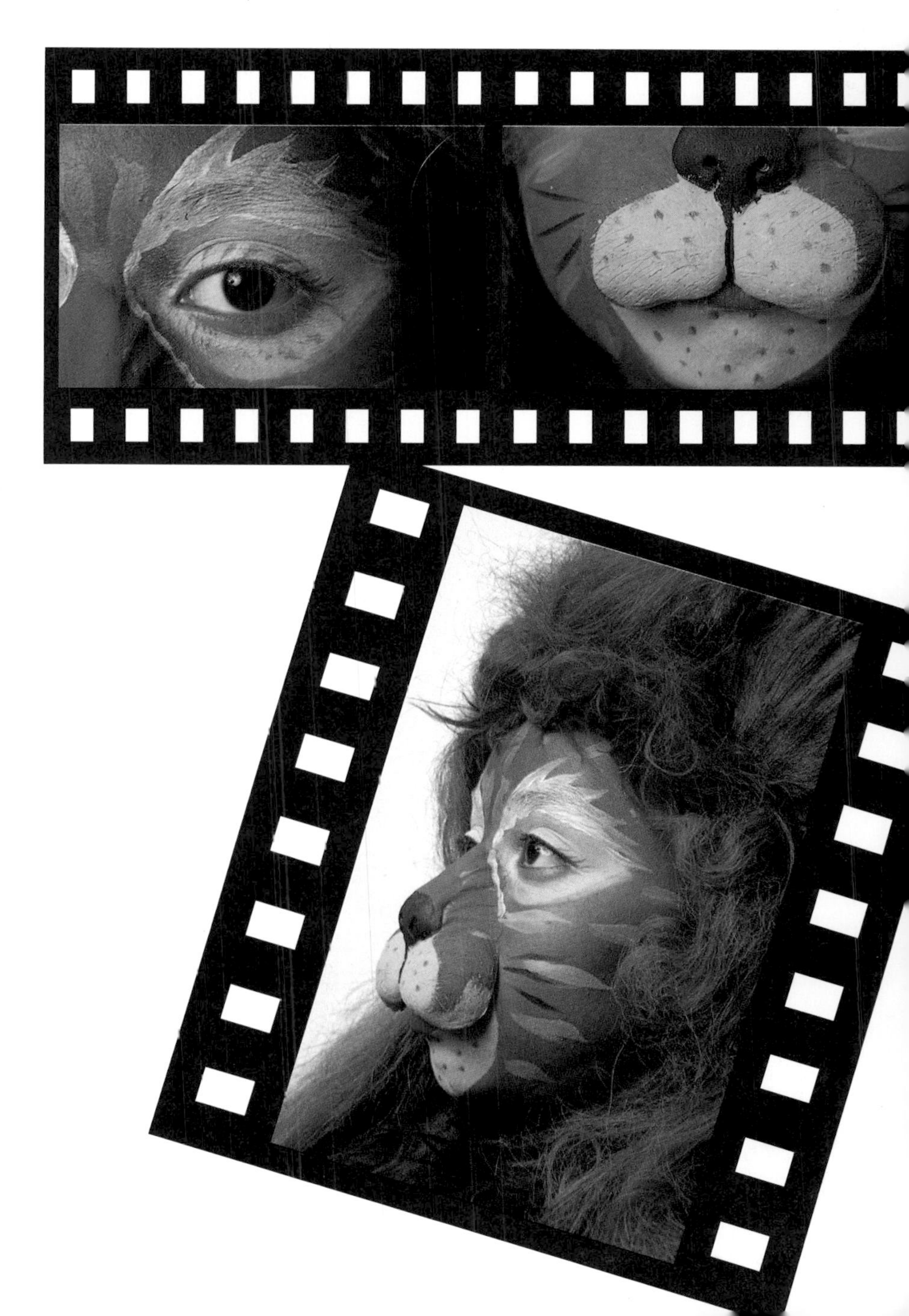

## Make-up

The make-up is water-based, so it is applied with a damp sponge or paintbrush, and it can be washed off later with soap and water. The process takes about 20 minutes. Look at the result when the model puts on the special lion's wig. A spray fixer ensures the make-up will stay in place and the performer is ready to go on stage. Isn't she splendid!

# Your own play

These Chinese children are enjoying their chance to perform on stage

Look at this group of children in China performing a play. They are obviously enjoying themselves. It's great fun to get together and put on a play. Perhaps you have taken part in a play at school. But if you have written your own play, why not perform it at home?

## Find some space

You will need space for rehearsals, so your first step is to decide just how much space you need. This depends on the number of actors, and on the play itself. You might even find it better to perform out of doors. Then call a meeting with your friends and decide who will play which part. It's a good idea to choose one person to be the director. You don't need to learn your lines before you start to rehearse – as long as there are enough scripts to go round.

## Taking on a character

If you have never acted before, imagine for a moment that you're going to play a wild, colourful character. Give some careful thought as to how you will play this character on stage. How will you behave with the people around you? What gestures will you make with your arms? How will you talk? What clothes will you wear? Begin to think in this way and you are building a new character.

## Dress the part

The children in this picture are wearing just jackets and hats to show which part they are playing. You don't need much in the way of costume, though wearing a special costume does help you to get into a role. It's not always easy to get hold of material to make costumes, so try to think of ways to adapt your own clothes. Ask the adults you know if they have any old clothes, hats or shoes they don't need. You might be able to adapt a shirt as shown on page 35.

Masks also help to create a character, and they can easily be made from card. Look at pages 57 and 127 for ideas. Will you need special sound effects? Look back to page 159 to see how to make your own. Learn to make use of objects around you – things which other people might be throwing away, or which you can borrow for your performance.

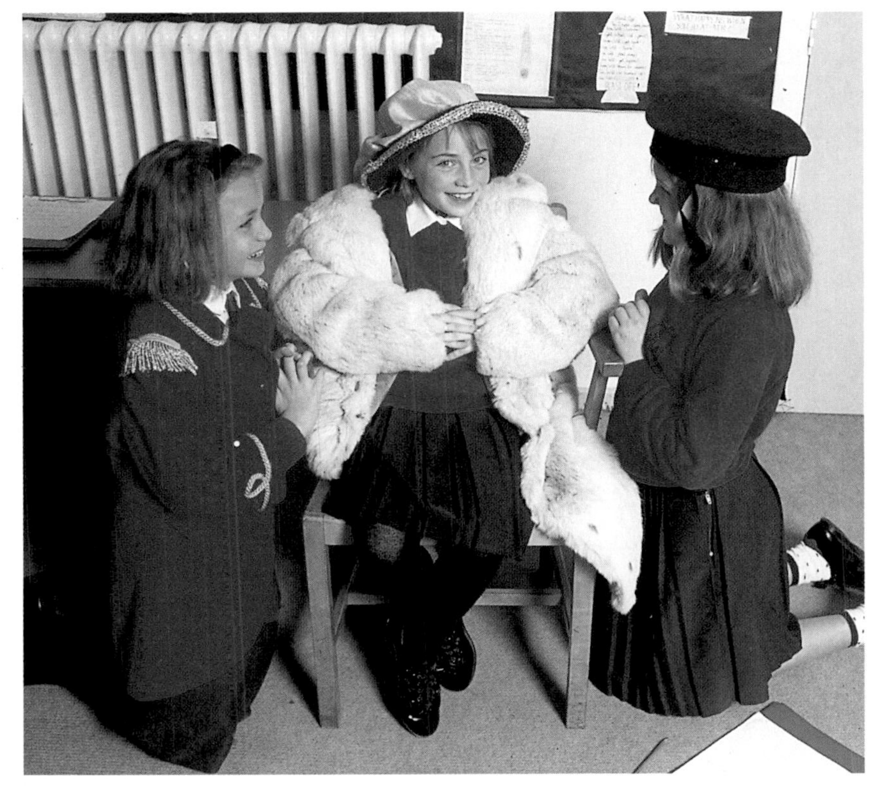

These children are ready for a simple performance

## Publicity

Don't forget to let people know when and where your play will be performed. Design a poster to advertise it. Choose a particular scene to illustrate your play. People are always attracted by eye-catching and colourful designs, so use bright colours. You might also like to make some tickets to issue before the performance. That way you will know how many people to expect and how many chairs to put out.

Good luck on your first night!

# A play in miniature

Did you make the toy theatre pictured on page 113? A toy theatre is very easy to make, and it's a good way of bringing the fun of a theatrical show into your own home. Try combining it with a colour wheel and sound effects to put on a very special show for your family and friends.

## First things first

First of all, you will need a script. Try writing your own using the tips given on page 168. Once you have a script, you will need to gather together some friends to help out. Ideally you will need four people – one to stand on either side of the toy theatre to move the rod puppets, one to control the colour wheel, and one to manage sound effects. Next you need to decide what sets you need, and what characters.

## The setting

It's useful to make a couple of different sets which can be slotted into your theatre. The underwater set you can see on page 149 was specially designed to fit into the toy theatre. Use seashells to decorate the floor of the set.

## The cast

Draw pictures of the characters you need onto card. Cut them out and tape them to sticks. You can operate the rod puppets from above or from the side of your toy theatre, depending on where you attach the stick. You may find the side approach easier – it's sometimes a bit difficult to peer into your theatre from above. Remember that you'll need to speak for the figures you're controlling. Jiggle them up and down when they speak so that the audience can tell which character is supposed to be speaking.

## Lights – and action!

The colour wheel shown on page 157 works well in throwing coloured light onto your miniature stage. Dim the lights and hold a torch behind each of the filters in turn. Decide which colour looks best for which scene. Think also about sound effects – blowing through a straw into a bowl of water makes a good sound for underwater scenes.

If you have several rehearsals you will have time to sort out any problems with lighting, sound, or with the script. Just like a real theatre, it's best to get everything right before raising the curtain!

# Glossary

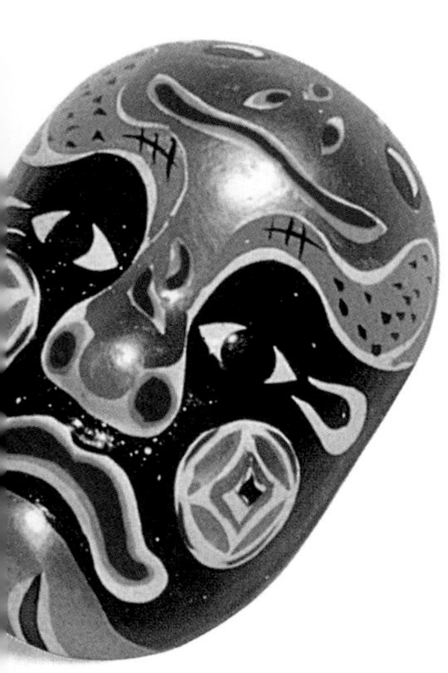

**absurd, theatre of the:** a style of drama that appeared in the 1950s, in which reality is turned upside-down.

**actor-director:** someone who both directs and acts in a play.

**amphitheatre:** a bowl-shaped theatre with seats for the audience rising steeply from the stage area.

**arena:** an open space, surrounded by seats, used for shows, plays or contests.

**audition:** a kind of trial during which performers demonstrate their skills.

**backcloth or backdrop:** painted scenery that hangs at the back of the stage. It might be plain, or painted with a scene.

**backstage:** the area behind the stage which is out of sight to the audience.

**balcony:** a seating area in the upper part of a theatre.

**box:** an enclosed seating area in an indoor theatre which holds a small party of people.

**carnival:** a celebration that takes place in the streets, with music, dancing and colourful costumes.

**cast:** the collective name given to all the actors in a production.

**character:** a person in a play; the part taken by an actor.

**chorus:** a group of singers, singing together; the music sung by a group of singers; a group of singers and dancers in Ancient Greek drama.

**classical:** refers to a play or other art form created according to set rules.

**comedy:** a funny play.

**costume:** the clothes worn by actors on stage.

**cue:** a signal to notify an actor to begin a speech.

**dance-drama:** a dramatic performance which is told through dance.

**dialogue:** the conversation between the characters in a play.

**director:** the person who controls the way in which a play is performed.

**downstage:** the front half of the stage, nearest to the audience.

**drama:** a play; the acting-out of scenes of conflict and of great emotional intensity.

**dressing room:** the room in which actors dress and prepare their make-up before a performance.

**ensemble:** a group of actors.

**fader:** a sliding knob that dims or brightens the stage lighting.

**farce:** a boisterous, knock-about comedy.

**flats:** the wooden frames which are used to make stage scenery.

**float:** a wagon or cart used as a moveable stage in outdoor performances.

**footlights:** lights which are positioned along the front of the stage.

**roustabout:** a member of the circus crew that puts up and takes down the circus tent.

**satyr play:** a comic play written by a writer of tragedies in Ancient Greece.

**scenario:** the outline of a play.

**scenery:** the stage decoration, including backdrop and flats, that shows the audience where a scene is taking place.

**score:** the written music of an opera or musical.

**script:** the written words of a play, or of an actor's part.

**set:** the surroundings in which the actors perform

**sketch:** a short, acted scene.

**slapstick:** a kind of comedy full of rough and tumble and jokes.

**sound effects:** the sounds deliberately created to make a performance more believable.

**special effects:** machinery, lighting or sound effects that give a particular result to add to the action on stage.

**spotlight:** a strong beam of light that lights up a small area of the stage.

**stage:** the area on which actors perform.

**stagehand:** a person who works behind the scenes in a theatre.

**stalls:** the seating area which faces the stage in a theatre building.

**stock:** see repertory.

**tableau, or tableau vivant:** a striking scene made by people holding a pose.

**theatre-in-the-round:** a performance in which the audience sits all round the stage.

**to fly:** to hang scenery over the stage and to lower it onto the acting area by means of ropes.

**tour:** the travels of a company of actors from town to town.

**tragedy:** a sad and serious play.

**trap door:** a covered hole in the stage through which actors can enter and exit.

**troupe:** a company of actors.

**typecast:** an actor who is typecast always acts the same kind of roles.

**upstage:** the back half the stage, furthest away from to the audience.

**wings:** flat pieces of scenery which are used at the sides of the stage.

# Index

# ACKNOWLEDGEMENTS

The publishers would like to thank the following for permission to reproduce these photographs:

The Ancient Art and Architecture Collection for Ancient Greek masks (page 12) and mosaic from Pompeii (page 14). Bibliotheque Nationale, Paris, for manuscript depicting the Valenciennes Passion Play, 1547, by Hubert Cailleau (pages 18-19); *Iphigenia* (page 42) and *The Imaginary Invalid* (page 43). Bildarchiv der Osterreichischen National Bibliothek, Vienna for stage set by Giacoma Torelli (pages 150-151). The Bridgeman Art Library for 'A Village Festival in Honour of St Hubert and St Anthony, 1632' by Pieter Breughel the Younger (pages 30-31); Grimaldi appearing in *Harlequin and the Golden Fish*, 1811 (pages 100-101); 'Pantomime' by Judy Joel (page 102) and Japanese actor with script (page 169). University of Bristol Theatre Collection for Khon drama performers, Thailand (page 66 and 67); miniature Chinese masks (page 128); etching of melodrama scene (page 132); *Under the Gaslight* (page 133); model set by Alan Tagg (pages 144-145 and 149); star trap with clown (page 152); the chariot race in *Ben-Hur*, 1902 (page 153); Kabuki performance by firelight (page 154) and costume designs (pages 145 and 161). The Trustees of the British Museum for scroll painting of open-air Chinese theatre (page 29). The Chatsworth Collection for two costume designs by Inigo Jones (page 89). The China National Tourist Office for acrobats (page 97). Christian Aid photo library for Indian actors (page 57). Compix for Peking Opera, Singapore (page 49); Kathakali performer (page 52-53); Trinidad Tent Theatre (page 79) and Benue State puppet troupe (page 84). Donald Cooper, Photostage for actors in rehearsal (page 173). Department for Education for children dressing up (page 181). Douglas Dickens for Spanish clowns as billposters (page 98); Chinese open-air theatre (page 29); Ennosuke Ichikawa in Kabuki (page 51); Kathakali performer (page 52); shadow play showing puppeteer (page 111); shadow play effect (page 111); Kathakali performance (pages 114-115 and 123); Nō play (page 124) and Kabuki theatre (page 148). Zoe Dominic for *Oresteia* (page 13); *The Return of Ulysses* (page 38); *The Life of Galileo* (page 136); construction of artificial tree (page 151) and lighting on stage for *Song and Dance* (page 156). Drottningholms Teatermuseum, Stockholm for 'Pantaloon's Serenade' (page 34). E.T. Archive for Globe theatre (page 41) and Japanese poster advertising *The Mikado* (page 75). Mary Evans for Ancient Greek vase painting of chorus (page 10); member of Ancient Greek chorus with lyre (page 10); vase painting showing satyr performers (pages 12-13); Hrotswitha (page 18); travelling entertainer (page 22); Brighella (page 36); Colombine (page 36); Pantaleone (page 37); Il Capitan Spezzaler (page 37); opera stage set (page 38-39); *The Marriage of Figaro* (pages 6-7 and 39); newspaper article reviewing *Aida* (page 73); scene from an English tragedy (page 80); Archellino (page 101); Japanese actors preparing for the stage (page 117); statue of a tragic actor (page 119); Ancient Greek masks (pages 126 and 127); Pepper's Ghost (page 152); an empty theatre (page 164) and Japanese theatre poster (page 165). The Robert Harding Picture Library for Jagannatha cart, India (page 91); Ancient Egyptian painting (page 119) and students at a Kathak school in India (page 122). The Horniman Museum and Gardens for Punch glove puppet (page 106); Judy glove puppet (page 107); Japanese Bunraku puppet (page 109); Turkish shadow puppet (page 111) and Garuda bird lamp (page 154). The Hulton Picture Library for Kyogen mask (pages 7 and 24); circus acrobats (page 96); clown (page 99); Ancient Greek statue of mime (page 138) and backstage preparations (page 170). The Hutchison Library for Bapende tribe, Zaire (pages 8-9); monkey dance, Bali (page 9); African minstrel (page 23); Kabuki performers (pages 46-47 and 51); Kathakali performer (page 53); Sudanese storyteller (page 56); *A Midsummer Night's Dream* (page 61); Peking Opera (page 62); Peking Opera performer (page 63); San Blas islanders (page 64); actor with theatre for community development, Tanzania (page 68); two pictures of San Blas islanders (page 70); carnival float, Malta (pages 86-87 and 92); carnival performers, Taiwan (page 93); Guadalupe festival (page 94); American puppeteer with marionette (page 104); Punch and Judy show, Leek (pages 106-107); actor on stage (page 120); Ugandan actors (page 121); woman painting mask (page 127); two pictures of Kabuki actor, Tokyo (page 129); children's theatre workshop in Tanzania (page 143); Festival of the Sun, Puru (pages 146-147); Balinese dance-drama (page 160); carnival audience, Malta (page 164) and actors rehearsing, Cameroon (page 176). The Ironbridge Gorge Museum, Shropshire for printing shop (page 95). Marquess of Bath, Longleat House, Wiltshire for manuscript by Henry Peachum showing *Titus Andronicus* (page 40). The MacQuitty International Photographic Collection for two pictures of Parisian street performer (page 65); backstage at a Peking Opera performance (page 161) and Nanking theatre (page 180). Mander & Mitchenson for pit entrance, Drury Lane (page 44); Interior of Drury Lane theatre in 1808 (page 45); Kabuki theatre (page 50); *Thark*, 1927 (page 78); portrait of Joseph Grimaldi (page 100); Poster advertising *The Streets of London* (page 133); *The Cherry Orchard* (page 134); *The Three Sisters* (pages 134-135); *Mother Courage and Her Children* (page 137) and Sarah Bernhardt (page 141); The Mansell Collection for backstage at a mystery play (page 20); mummers in banqueting hall, Derbyshire (page 26); Oberammergau Passion Play, 1870 (page 54) and facial expressions (pages 124 and 125). Richard Mildenhall for three pictures depicting *The Little Clay Cart* (pages 16 and 17). G. Namur, Lalance for jigging puppets (page 105). National Gallery, London for 'Sir Henry Unton' (page 88). Sue Adler/The Performing Arts Library for street performers, London (page 64). Clive Barda/The Performing Arts Library for *Carmen* (pages 48-49); *The Comedy of Errors* (page 59); scene from *Carousel* (page 74); scenery construction (page 150); sound effects (158); two pictures of Michael Crawford preparing for *Phantom of the Opera* (page 162); prompter (page 171); actors rehearsing *The Wizard of Oz* (pages 176-177) and performance of *The Wizard of Oz* (page 177). Pollock's Toy Museum for etching depicting toy theatre performance (page 112); large toy theatre, set for *Sleeping Beauty* (page 112) and toy theatre characters from *Oliver Twist* (page 112). The Royal Shakespeare Company for *The Winter's Tale* (page 61). Staatliche Museen Preussischer Kulturbesitz, Berlin for vase painting (page 15). John Massey Stewart for Obraztsov Puppet Theatre (page 76). Strand Lighting Ltd for colour call scrollers (page 74 and 75); lighting control board (page 147); and prelude spotlight (page 156). Toneelmuseum, Amsterdam for a box at the Schouwburg (page 45). Topham Picture Source for mystery play (page 21); *Romeo and Juliet* (pages 60-61); *Starlight Express* performers (page 75); Mardi Gras float (page 93); English Civil War Society (pages 94-95); Leo McKern (page 116); actors on stage (page 117); Australian Aborigines (page 118); Leo Mckern (page 130); mime with puppet (page 138); Marcel Marceux (page 139); two pictures of Laurence Olivier (page 140); children's musical *Lollypops* (page 142); actors practising movement (page 143); set designer and director with model set (page 148); actors discussing costume designs (page 160) and *Aida* (pages 172-173). Unicef for masked dancer, Bhutan (page 126). The Board of Trustees of the Victoria and Albert Museum for The Triumph of Isabella, Brussels, 1615, by Daniel van Alsloot (page 90); plate of fish (page 131) and Max Reinhardt's 1911 production of *The Miracle* (pages 174-175). Reg Wilson for Nō theatre (pages 24-25); interior of RSC, Stratford-upon-Avon (page 58); Grace Bumbry (page 73); *It Runs in the Family* (page 79); *Death of a Salesman* (page 81); *Endgame* (page 82); *Waiting for Godot* (pages 82-83); marionettes (page 104) and Japanese Bunraku performance (page 108). Zefa Library for Epidaurus theatre (page 11); Oberammergau 'Last Supper' (pages 54-55); opera at Verona arena (page 72); Peking Opera in Thailand (page 85) and Teatro Olimpico (page 146).

The publishers would also like to give special thanks to Gina Brierley, Dragan Cortan, Dauphine's of Bristol, Christopher Robinson at the Bristol University Theatre Collection and John Twine Lighting Hire, Bath for the loan of items for photography and to Allen Bills at Dauphine's of Bristol for advice and for making-up the model on pages 178-179 to be photographed.